Praise for *Leather Soul*

'Part autobiography, part paean to football. Murphy writes in a way that will draw in fan and non-fan alike.'
Michael Rowland, ABC News Breakfast presenter

'[An] honest, moving and brutally self-aware account.'
Bill Perrett, The Sydney Morning Herald

'*Leather Soul* paints a poignant picture of a man struggling to overcome the enormity of missing out on the game of his life.'
Kate O'Halloran, The Guardian

'Bob Murphy's got a great story to tell, and he does it pretty damn well. He was an exceptional footballer. Lucky lad, he's an exceptional writer too. *Leather Soul* is … superb.'
Paul Amy, Leader Newspapers and Inside Football

'There is only one Bob Murphy.'
Martin Flanagan

Bob Murphy
Leather Soul

A half-back flanker's rhythm and blues

NERO

Published by Nero,
an imprint of Schwartz Publishing Pty Ltd
Level 1, 221 Drummond Street
Carlton VIC 3053, Australia
enquiries@blackincbooks.com
www.nerobooks.com

Copyright © Robert D. Murphy 2018
This edition published in 2019
Robert D. Murphy asserts his right to be known as the author of this work.

ALL RIGHTS RESERVED.
No part of this publication may be reproduced, stored in a retrieval system, or transmitted in any form by any means electronic, mechanical, photocopying, recording or otherwise without the prior consent of the publishers.

9781760641412 (paperback)
9781743820568 (ebook)

A catalogue record for this book is available from the National Library of Australia

Cover design by Peter Long
Illustrations by Jim Pavlidis

Photographs courtesy of AFL Media ('Leading the boys out'); Adrian Brown ('A quiet beer'); Cameron Spencer / AFL Media / Stringer ('Being swept away'); Craig Johnstone ('Match committee for the Rockdogs'); Darrian Traynor / AFL Media / Stringer ('A Bulldog prayer'); George Salpigtidis / Newspix ('Lifting weights is optional'); Michael Klein / Newspix ('You boo him, you boo all of us', 'On some days it still hurts', 'A couple of proud Bulldogs'); Michael Wilson / AFL Media / Stringer ('Showing my true colours'); Quinn Rooney / Getty ('The pain of losing', 'Sealed with a drunken kiss', 'A sea of red, white and blue'); Ryan Pierse / Getty ('We hug a lot'); Stephen Harman / Newspix ('Playing for the Big V'); Wayne Ludbey / Newspix ('A medal for al those players'). All other photographs courtesy of Robert D. Murphy.

Through his passion and devotion, and his astounding performances on and off the field, Bob Murphy led the Western Bulldogs to glory. When Bob took over the captaincy, the club was in disarray and lacked player leadership. In this time of need, Bob stepped up to the challenge. We draped a cape around his neck and asked him to draw on all of his talents. He would ultimately connect the Western Bulldogs Football Club to itself.

Sometimes we are lucky to stumble upon people in our lives. Other times we are blessed. I am both of these in relation to Bob. We are all prospecting in our journey through life, and the day we met Bob Murphy, we struck gold.

You may not know Bob personally, but in these pages he gives a little bit of himself to each and every one of you. As you read, imagine he has lent you his weathered denim jacket. Off he rolls in his flannel, and on you both rock.

Enjoy the ride!
Luke Beveridge

Foreword
by Martin Flanagan

George Bernard Shaw famously declared, 'Those who can, do; those who can't, teach.' In sport, this generally translates as: 'Those who can, play; those who can't, write about it.' So, in talking about a new book to do with sport, it is important to note that there is not one tradition of sports writing, but two.

The first and most common tradition is that of the observer, the (hopefully) well-informed spectator. In sports writing, as in all non-fiction writing, it is crucial for the writer to know and identify where they sit in relation to their subject. As the great American photographer Ansel Adams said of his art, 'A good photograph is knowing where to stand.' Years ago, I had a difference of opinion with a colleague about whether journalists are entitled to question the courage of AFL players. She said courage was part of the game, therefore writers had the right to comment on whether or not they believed individual players possessed it. I am fundamentally opposed to that view. I've twice seen my wife give birth – I know what it looks like, but I'm not going to say I know what it feels like. Sports writers in this first tradition are people with a practised eye, informed by what they are told by the participants, but essentially remaining spectators. The great sports writers in this tradition know that – it's part of the fidelity, the precision, of their art.

The second, much rarer category of sports writers is players or athletes who also happen to be writers. No-one can define good writing, but one important attribute is clearly originality, both of perspective and of expression. It has something to do with putting life on the page in the same way that artists do when they sketch a likeness. American runner Kenny Moore, English cricketer Peter Roebuck, Irish soccer player Eamon Dunphy, Australian footballer Brent Crosswell and Australian boxer Mischa Merz are notable examples of athletes who are also writers. Doubly gifted, these individuals have the ability to convey what happens in their sports in a way that takes you beyond appearances, beyond speculation, into the internal world of the participant or performer. The difference between the two traditions can be as great as the difference between a simple account of a small girl sitting beside a tree talking to herself, and *Alice in Wonderland*.

Leather Soul stands squarely in this second tradition of sports writing. For as long as I have known Bob Murphy, he has been wholly original in his perceptions and the way that he expresses them. He is as natural in this as he was in the way he played the game. One of my favourite quotes about art comes from jazz great Duke Ellington: 'It don't mean a thing, if it ain't got that swing.' Bob's writing has swing, though I wouldn't necessarily liken Bob's writing to jazz – he puts me more in mind of an Irish tin-whistle player. In an important and necessary sense, his writing is simple – he has that immediately recognisable individual quality that the Irish call 'voice'. Consistent with this is the fact he is always going his own way, over the hills and far away, illustrating a lot of what he has to say with insights into Australia's national game and the people who populate it. As a player, he had superb balance – so, too, as a writer: balance in seeing deep into the game while knowing, at the same time, it's only a game; balance in knowing that the game has a hard edge (no-one writes better about fear) but never in a way that coarsens his perceptions of his fellow players. He's poignant, he's light, he's serious, he's bright. He's going his own merry way, providing a view you won't get anywhere else. I'm here to tell you there is only one Bob Murphy.

Martin Flanagan
Melbourne, May 2018

Player Profile

Name: Robert Daniel Murphy

Height: 187cm

Weight: 83kg

Position: Flanker

Nicknames: Butch, The Mouth, Blue 5

Toughest opponent: Steve Johnson / Max Hudghton

Favourite movie: *Field of Dreams*

Favourite dish to cook: Toasted sandwiches

Favourite song: 'Thunder Road' by Bruce Springsteen

Favourite holiday destination: Bangalow

Favourite album: *Exile on Main St* (Rolling Stones)

Hidden skill: Backyard cricket trick ball

Bad habit: Winnebago driving

Dream dinner guests: Tim Ross, Rob Sitch, Julia Zemiro, Andy Kelly, Don Walker

Contents

Foreword by Martin Flanagan		vii
Prologue		1
1	Mum Was a Nun and Dad Was a Priest	5
2	Footy in the Schoolyard	17
3	I Met a Girl in High School	23
Wednesday, 15 October 2014: Peter Gordon's place		33
4	Football's Chook Raffle	37
Tuesday, 24 February 2015: Whitten Oval, training session		53
5	Conscripts and Volunteers	57
6	Must Be the Irish in Me	61
Saturday, 2 May 2015: Sydney, preparing to take on the Swans		67
7	Pre-Season Torture Camp	77
8	Playing Tall	85
Saturday, 12 September 2015: Adelaide		91

9	Finding My Voice	93
	Sunday, 14 January 2016: Northcote	103
10	My Knee Goes 'Pop'	107
	Sunday, 10 April 2016: Western Bulldogs v. Hawthorn, Etihad Stadium	115
11	The Apprenticeship	119
	Monday, 11 April 2016: Northcote	127
12	The Hot Seat	129
	Sunday, 29 May 2016: Palm Springs, California	141
13	Bottoming Out	143
	Thursday, 14 July 2016: Whitten Oval	149
	Monday, 5 September 2016: Returning from the Pyrenees	155
	Thursday, 29 September 2016: Whitten Oval, final training session	159
	Saturday, 1 October 2016: The MCG, Grand Final Day	163
14	A Stadium Holds Its Breath	171
	Thursday, 23 March 2017: Northcote	183
15	You Don't Get to Choose Your Own Nickname	193
	Saturday, 25 March 2017: Northcote	203

16 We Are Family	207
Thursday, 13 April 2017: Captain's run	**217**
17 Blokes I Loved Playing Against	225
Friday, 11 August 2017: Western Bulldogs v. GWS, Docklands, 12-minute mark, second quarter (WB 28, GWS 35)	**237**
18 Characters I Loved Playing With	239
Saturday, 19 August 2017: Dreary Ballarat	**263**
19 Leadership and All That	269
Friday, 25 August 2017: Hawthorn v. Western Bulldogs, Etihad Stadium	**275**
20 The End	279
Afterword by Gerard Whateley	293
Acknowledgements	297

There are days when you could give it up.
There are days when you could fly.

Mike Brady, 'Up There Cazaly'

Prologue

On Grand Final Day 2016, I wake up hungover.

Last night, Bulldogs president Peter Gordon held a gathering at his sprawling Hawthorn home for a bunch of influential Bulldogs people from days gone by and their partners. You could feel a deep sense of camaraderie in the room, a testament to the healing that has taken place at the club since Luke Beveridge took over as coach at the end of 2014.

Wine, mixed with a heady anticipation that only the oldest Bulldogs in the room had known previously, filled the room with a palpable buzz. Speeches were given and stories were swapped, but the backdrop was one simple question: what will tomorrow bring for the Bulldogs clan? It was hard not to get swept up in the enormity of what might happen in the next 24 hours. Eventually only the Gordons and the Murphys remained. But Santa only comes if little children go to sleep, and finally even we had to go home.

Since I was a little boy kicking a ball into the powerlines outside our house in Warragul, anticipating which way it would bounce when it returned to earth and darting in that direction, this is all I'd dreamed of. Since I first walked onto Whitten Oval as a 17-year-old, I've yearned for my beloved club to reach a grand final. And tomorrow they're finally there: their first grand final in 55 years, with the prospect of their first premiership in 62 seasons, just the second in the Bulldogs' history.

And here I am, lying in bed with a hangover.

A knee injury back in April pulled me out of this momentous season. I can't help feeling I've been cheated out of my destiny, that I've dedicated a good chunk of my heart, body and soul to my football club and just as we're about to walk into the sunshine, I'm shackled in the shadows. As they say, there are mixed emotions.

I spend the morning shuffling around the house, trying to keep busy. I take my dog, Arthur, for a walk and pick up coffees from my local café. Burning time.

But now it's time to get ready, to put on my match day clothes. I decide to wear my playing jumper under my club polo shirt and jacket. It's a symbol. I want to be as close to the players as I possibly can. I am with them, supporting them, even if I am not one of them on the field today. They are going into battle and I am not. For me, there will be no corked thigh, no cut above the brow, no hip and shoulders to absorb. But wearing the jumper is my way of putting the war paint on nonetheless.

I stand in our bedroom looking out the window and take a moment to myself. In the days leading up to today, I've felt numb, and I think there is a part of me that wants to indulge in the pain of putting on my team's colours even though I can't play. To really feel it.

Just as I lift my sacred Bulldogs jumper over my head and my arms slip through the holes, Justine walks in. A heavy silence fills the room: a man and his wife, both knowing there is nothing to say that will make things better.

After a moment, Justine leaves in tears.

It's going to be a hell of a day.

1

Mum Was a Nun and Dad Was a Priest

I adore the smell of football leather. For me, it's like time travel. One whiff and I'm whisked away on a magic carpet ride, back to my childhood bedroom: I'm nine years old, lying awake in bed with my football, daydreaming. My nine-year-old self couldn't care less about the stresses of professional life, played out in the public eye. The thought that he'll one day become an AFL player is enough to have him jumping on his bed with joy, before heading out to the backyard to start another game in his imagination.

That's all the perspective I usually need. A sniff of a footy. Cheap therapy.

I was at my teammate and close friend Will Minson's country wedding not so long ago, and a few hours before the ceremony I found one of his brothers and groomsmen, Hugh, polishing a well-loved pair of RM Williams boots with Dubbin and a tattered rag. It almost reduced me to tears. It reminded me of my dad.

When I first started playing football as a little kid, Dad would clean my boots on the Friday night before we played the following morning. Using a tattered cloth just like Hugh's, Dad would massage oily resin into the leather to protect them from the mud and the rain. I didn't think about it much at the time – what nine-year-old would? That's just what Dad used to do.

We'd get up the next morning, just the two of us, and travel through the wind, rain and sometimes fog to one of the little satellite towns around Warragul for that week's game. Once there, my coach, Frank Ahern, would bring me and the other kids in tight to reiterate his coaching philosophy: 'Kick it into the open spaces and be prepared to run!' We'd go out and play our hearts out, but most of us had our long-sleeved jumpers pulled down over our fingers to battle the cold.

When I see a tin of Dubbin now, I see things a whole lot differently. The thought of that simple ritual moves me. He's a kind and patient man, my father. I've learnt a lot from him, absorbed so many of his ways, but as I get older I think perhaps the thing he's taught me most is the importance of ceremony and ritual. Not that he would say this kind of thing out loud – although he's an ex-priest, Dad is no preacher – but the same reverence we have for a wedding, baptism or funeral can be brought to a simple autumn morning or the ritual of making your wife a cup of coffee. These little things are just as important, and sometimes we need to slow down to appreciate them.

As a former man of the cloth, Dad was pretty handy with a tattered rag: my boots were always clean. Dad joined the seminary at 17, soon after he lost both his parents – in a single year. He had an older brother, Maurice, but because of the nine-year age gap between them, Dad had been like a single child growing up. Having lost his folks at such a young and impressionable age, Dad saw the seminary more like a surrogate family than a career path. I'm not sure if Dad saw his time in the priesthood as a calling – I've never heard him use that phrase – but it could have been. Mum and Dad still go to church, but they aren't particularly pious.

There's often a central story in family life – an event, a romance or a tragedy – around which everything else is built. In our family, it was Mum and Dad's love story. Mum was a nun and Dad was a priest – or, rather, they had been. Both left their religious orders after they met and fell in love. A story full of bravery and romance, we held it up on a pedestal. We still do. Back in the early 1990s though, us kids were more preoccupied with the details. Like, 'Hey, Mum, did you pash Dad when he was a priest?' Cheeky devil, I bet she did. Nothing was ever confirmed.

Mum was not the only nun in her family – three of her sisters also became nuns, but Mum told me that she never quite fit in with the strict rules and was restless for much of her time at the convent.

When Mum and Dad got married, they swiftly moved to Alice Springs. Actually, even further than that – Yulara, which is a good five hours from Alice. A classic Catholic story: go through a life-changing event, seek solace in the desert. Jesus 101. In Yulara, Mum and Dad worked as teachers in the Indigenous community. It was there that my brother, Ben, was born and then, almost a year later to the day, my sister, Bridget. The four of them lived in the Northern Territory for four years. So many kitchen table yarns in our home growing up hailed from that time in the Red Centre.

Even though I didn't feature in those stories, they were in my blood.

One day Mum fainted somewhere near Uluru and discovered she was pregnant again (oops) with me, and at that point my parents decided to return to Victoria to be closer to family. Dad's brother, Maurice – Maurie to us kids – lived in Ballarat with his wife, Mary, and their nine children.

So Mum and Dad set up home in Ballarat. Dad studied librarianship at St Patrick's College and Ben and Bridget started school at St Columba's. And on 9 June 1982 at 6 pm, I came along. Mum says that in the hospital they wrapped me up and handed me to Dad, and I gently stroked his face with my right hand. I don't know if that really happened, but I like the image of it.

Money must have been tight back then, with Dad studying and Mum tending to us kids; I'm sure friends and family helped us make ends meet. We only lived in Ballarat for a short while, so my memory of it is a bit patchy, but I still have some clear recollections from that time. I learnt to ride a bike out the front of our three-bedroom cream-brick home, and I can vividly picture our backyard on Sherrard Street, with the cricket pitch gently sloping away from the right-hander.

Ben is five years older than me, and like most boys of that era he was pretty obsessed with cricket and footy. It must have been frustrating for him trying to teach his three-year-old brother how to play cricket, because I'd really taken to heart the rule of staying in my crease. No matter what happened, whether he bowled me middle stump or caught me with a diving catch, I was stubborn in my belief that if I remained in my crease I couldn't be dismissed.

One of the games we played as kids was not as common as cricket or footy, but perhaps sums up the spirit of the times. I'm four years younger than Bridget, and my siblings must have sometimes found it a drag to have me around them all the time. So they devised a game where the aim was simply both of them running off on me. One of them would look at the other and then yell out 'S.P.I. on Robbie!' I guess what they meant was 'Spy on Robbie', but it didn't really matter how you spelt it. The result was always the same: 'S.P.I. on Robbie' was called, they ran off, I bawled my eyes out, and Mum came outside and flipped out. When I recall the shrieks of joy from my siblings whenever a game of 'S.P.I. on Robbie' took flight, it still sends a shiver down my spine.

I spent lots of time at my cousins' house and was in awe of them all, especially Dominic. He was tall, had a mullet and played basketball. In 1985 he was it, as far as I was concerned. My cousins had a German Shepherd called Tess. I've always liked German Shepherds, and I put that down to my time with her.

I also remember Ballarat's Lake Wendouree. The lake was full then and it was lined by big, elegant, overhanging trees and a sandy path. Mum told me she would walk me around the lake and I'd ride my little bike with training wheels the whole way. Apparently, I was bribed with lollies to keep going when I got puffed out.

Ballarat was good to me and my family; whenever I visit I get a warm feeling of nostalgia when I see the deep bluestone drains that line the streets.

*

LEATHER SOUL

In 1986 Dad got a job in Warragul as the regional librarian. We moved there not knowing anyone from Warragul or anything about the place. And it was only once we'd arrived that I realised I'd left my favourite Mr. T figurine in Ballarat. Dominic went searching for it, and he found it under the veranda where I said it would be. My cousin was kind enough to send it on to Warragul. I loved that plastic doll with all my heart. I was three-and-a-half years old.

We rented a house on Biram Drive, which was good for Mum because she had a new job at the Catholic secondary school, Marist Sion, which was just up the hill.

Mum was one of 14 children, so to have found a town in Victoria without one of her brothers or sisters living in it was quite an achievement. I remember going to a family reunion for Mum's side up near Bendigo somewhere: it looked like a musical festival for Irish Catholics. Kids were scattered everywhere like mice and all the adults pretty much looked the same and even chewed their food in a similar fashion.

Dad worked at the library in the heart of town, and Ben and Bridget were the new kids at St Joseph's Primary School. I spent my days in the care of a wonderful lady named Mary Harriet. She had a house, not too far away from our rental, that was on a couple of acres close to the edge of town. Mary guided me on all kinds of adventures – milking cows, trips to the indoor pool at Moe, watching Ray Martin on daytime TV... I wasn't that into Ray, but everything else we did was tops.

At home, us kids were left to our own devices a lot, as you might expect with both parents working full-time jobs. I'm amazed at how many hours of entertainment my brother and I could get out of twisting and folding a pair of Dad's thick, red Explorer socks into a makeshift football and practising our goal-kicking with it. We would adjust the sliding door of the lounge room to increase the degree of difficulty. We got quite good, although in the great tradition of Australian family life, some of Mum's vases were destroyed in the pursuit of goal-kicking supremacy.

One afternoon in that first year of our time in Warragul, when I was entertaining myself out the front of the house, I jumped into the front seat of Mum's beaten-up old Kingswood, which was parked in the driveway, and accidentally knocked the handbrake off. The car started to roll gently towards the street. I panicked, jumped out and tried to push against the Kingswood's momentum. That's what they call 'cock-eyed optimism'. I couldn't keep the car from rolling away and got myself stuck half in the car, half out. I broke a piece of my scapula. It was a close call, but I don't remember there being a big song and dance about it.

All in all, we had good times in Biram Drive, but Warragul didn't really feel like home until we moved to the other side of town: to 186 Albert Road, a simple, three-bedroom, sandy-coloured brick home with a rumpus room and a big backyard. Our home. I don't think there was much of a garden when we arrived, but Mum took to it with the vigour of a true green thumb and created a lush suburban sanctuary. Pavers were laid, ponds were excavated, compost was king.

And of course, there was a cricket pitch. Unlike the one we had in Ballarat, this pitch sloped away from the left-hander – no good for me, but great for my brother's outswinger. Ben was a right-handed batsman, whereas I was a lefty, so the conditions really suited him. I'd be okay though, as long as I stayed in my crease.

There was a nectarine tree in the backyard that bore fruit in the summer, and we'd eat nectarines until we got sick. Out the front there was a spindly native tree alongside a power pole, the perfect footy goals. But the real jewel of 186 Albert Road was the six-metre-high gum tree in the middle of the lawn in the front yard. This tree was the perfect 'climber', and when you got up as high as we did, you could look back down over much of the town. We gave the tree the moniker 'Herbie', after the VW bug that had a mind of its own, and many a plan was hatched high up in his branches.

Like all kids, we had some rules and boundaries, but if I could sum up my childhood in one word, it would be 'freedom'.

One day, when I was about seven, I decided to jump the back fence and go looking for an adventure or someone to play with. I landed in our neighbour's yard, walked casually through to Normanby Street, took a left, walked 50 metres and found a bunch of kids having a game of cricket in their front yard. That was the Pitts' house and they had two boys, David and Stephen, who were close to my age. I reckon I played 3000 Test matches in the Pitts' front yard since that day. The Pitt boys wouldn't stand for my 'But I'm in my crease!' rubbish though. I remain good friends with both of them to this day.

By then, school was a big part of my routine, but life was still one long lunchtime as far as I was concerned. If I wasn't playing cricket, I was on my bike doing jumps over driveways. If it was a summer day, I was down at the pool with my mates moving in a swarm around the lap and diving pools, always keeping an eye on the ten-metre tower that loomed over us, and slowly building up the courage to one day jump from it ourselves. It sounds disgusting now, but with the loose change I swindled from Mum and Dad for a day at the pool, I'd sometimes buy a toffee apple bar or a killer python snake, cram it in my mouth in one go, and immediately get back in the pool – jumping off the diving boards, perfecting my bombs. The 'Jackie', the 'Coffin', the 'Can Opener': I'd execute all of these with a mouth full of my favoured confectionary. The pool water would wash in and slosh about, creating sugary, chlorinated glory. I loved it.

If this all sounds a bit like an episode of *The Wonder Years* or a sequel to *The Sandlot*, well, that's kind of how I remember it. Filtered through a golden lens of games, laughter, scraped knees, bags of lollies, sunburn and the art of knocking on people's front doors and running off. Life was fun, easy, breezy. It was almost completely stress-free.

Almost, but not quite. One weekend we spent Sunday visiting our cousins from Mum's side of the family, in Dandenong, and we arrived back in Warragul quite late. Ben, Bridget and myself were all asleep in the back seat and had to be carried into the house and put in our beds (is there anything better?). Us sleepy kids had no idea, but that night Mum discovered our beloved pet cat, Shaka (as in Shaka Zulu) dead on the side of the road at the front of our house. Poor old Shaka had been hit by a car. Once us kids were safely in bed, Mum gave Dad a blunt instruction: 'Go and bury the cat.'

Oblivious, we woke up the next morning and started getting ready for school. I heard a noise in the backyard and went to see what was happening. There I found Mum and Bridget staring down at what can only be described as a horrific scene.

Dad's attempt to bury the cat had come up a bit short. Battling poor light, fatigue and maybe a shiraz or two, Dad had buried the front half of Shaka (head, chest and arms) in a shallow grave, but left the back half sticking out of the ground. I didn't understand it at the time, but obviously rigor mortis had set in. Shaka's rear was sticking out of the ground, pointing stiffly towards the sky. His tail was rigid – tall and straight like the handle of a golf club.

An air of panic already filled the backyard, but things were about to get worse. In a brave attempt to fix the problem and start again, dear old Mum decided she would take Shaka by the tail and lift him out of the dirt. With hindsight, I think Mum might concede this exhumation plan wasn't entirely thought through.

As Mum took hold of Shaka and put her back into it, the fur from his tail came off as clean as the sock off a brand-new pitching wedge. Mum took a step back, almost stumbled, and stood there in shock, with the fur of Shaka's tail still in her hand. The cat, complete with exposed tailbone, remained in the ground. It was a traumatic moment for everyone, and I include Shaka in that. Screams of remorse and hilarity from Mum and Bridget ensued. I just stood there in stunned silence. It was quite a scene.

While I remembered this episode clearly, when I came to write about the Shaka incident, I started to wonder if I'd possibly embellished the story in my mind a bit. So I rang Bridget and said, 'Look, this is my memory of what happened that day, but I was quite young – what's your recollection of it?'

She replied without hesitation. 'No, that's exactly what happened.'

I'm pleased to report that eventually Shaka was given a proper burial in the backyard, affording him the dignity and respect he deserved. We replaced him with a much more placid cat named Paddy.

Paddy lived a long life without major incident, until the day Dad burst through the front door, upset and a little frantic, and declared, 'I've killed the cat.' Paddy had been sunning himself on

the driveway and didn't quite get out of the way when Dad came home from work.

We didn't replace Paddy, which was probably wise.

We mightn't have had the best luck with our domestic felines, but they were greatly loved. And we were also fans of bigger cats: the Richmond Tigers. Dad had been born supporting Richmond and Ben and I followed in his footsteps. My favourite player was Wayne Campbell: I had his number 9 on my Tigers jumper. Bridget barracked for a few teams over the years; Mum had a soft spot for Collingwood. Curiously, in one of our family photos from 1985, Bridget is wearing a Footscray Bulldogs scarf. We never really got to the bottom of how that came about, but I like its serendipity. We were a football family: it was quite common for us to pile into the car and drive down to Waverley Park to watch AFL games, but we were just as likely to watch the local football league, parking our car at Western Park and tooting the horn with each goal.

A football family, yes, but there was plenty else that kept us occupied. In particular, there were always books around the house. Maybe because Dad was a librarian and Mum was a teacher, we were always encouraged to read. I have fond memories of Dad reading Roald Dahl novels to me before bed. My favourite was *James and the Giant Peach*. The words evoked such imagery in my head that if I closed my eyes as Dad read, I could transport myself onto the peach with James. I think I probably got my love of words and stories from that time.

2

Footy in the Schoolyard

'Keep your feet' is one of the greatest sayings in the football vernacular.

At St Joseph's in Warragul, where I went to school, it had extra resonance. You see, we didn't have a footy oval as such; we had a gravel car park. For the kids at St Joe's, 'keeping your feet' wasn't just about staying in the contest, it was the difference between keeping the skin on your hands and knees and going home looking like you'd fallen off your bike racing down a hill. I can still remember looking down at my hands in horror after being tackled during a lunchtime game, to see that loose stones had not only pierced the skin, but lodged themselves deep beneath it. We played for keeps, as they say.

A red brick retaining wall separated the two tiers of the car park; the bottom level was reserved for the serious football, while the top level was for the little kids. The 'footy ground', if you could call it that, was inhabited by a motley crew of big kids, small kids, fast kids, slow kids and everyone in-between. But I don't remember any girls playing, which I hope is different in primary schools these days.

Captains were nominated and everyone else would stand with their backs to the red brick wall. The playground can be a brutal place, and St Joe's was no different. If you could play, you were picked early; if you were no good, you were left sweating until the very end. It was a long wait for some of my classmates. One by one, players were picked until no-one was left; only then would the game begin.

I was never one of the big kids on the footy field or in the schoolyard, but I always got picked early. I took to most sports quite naturally and always had a feel for the game. Dad says that in the first game I ever played for the 'Colts', as a nine-year-old, I spent the first seven or eight minutes just watching from outside the pack. Up until then, I'd only played basketball and Dad wondered if I might be too timid for football. Then the ball jarred loose and I swooped on it, took it in my hands, dodged through the traffic and found a teammate with a right-foot pass. Dad remembers thinking, 'He's got it, he's got the gift.' But in the car park of St Joe's, I wasn't aware of any of that.

The goals at one end were imaginary, the car park narrowing to a driveway that led to the bitumen court which our parents' cars would pass through come 3.30 pm. At the other end was the rear of the church. Two columns of stained-glass windows stood tall and proud, ascending to the heavens and filtering the sun's rays into multicoloured light that bathed the faces of the devoted each Sunday at Mass. This was of no interest to us – at lunchtime those holy windows were simply the most perfect goalposts.

We had two mantras on that field at St Joe's: 'Keep your feet' and 'Don't hit the post.'

Much to the annoyance of Father McCartin and our principal, Brian Robertson, we hit the post regularly and broke plenty of the church's windows.

Running along one side of the field was the red brick wall, and along the other was a cyclone fence that separated the schoolyard from the rest of the world. When I think about that fence now, I think of Adam 'Blacky' Blackwood and I shudder. Blacky was a year older than me, but he was almost a foot shorter – and I wasn't tall. He may have been short, but he was the most feared boy on the playground. Stocky and fierce, Blacky had a few older brothers; despite being pretty much our age, he seemed to have seen more than we had. I was scared of Blacky. He was strong like a bull. If he caught you in a tackle anywhere near the cyclone fence, you could be pretty sure he'd swing you into it.

Blacky wasn't the only kid on that playground with a reputation. There were a lot of talented footballers on that gravel. By the time I got to Grade 5, our school football team was crowned the best in the state – quite an accomplishment for a smallish country school with no oval. Our teacher and football coach that year was Andrew Osler, and he fired our imaginations with a David versus Goliath spirit: 'The country kids without an oval against the big, fancy city kids with their lush green grass!' It was that kind of vibe, and we latched onto it with glee. I was still in Grade 5 at the time and the team was mostly Grade 6s. I was starting to gain a reputation in the schoolyard as a kid that could play.

For schoolkids, we were a bloody good team and we had some impressive local pedigree too. Leigh Baldry was probably the best player in our gang. He was a rover, tough and creative, the son of Victorian cricketer Bob Baldry. Ben 'Killer' Kilday was the son of Terry, a local electrician who always wore shorts in winter and had been a local star playing as a centre half-forward. Terry was a gun and his boy Ben was too. With flaming red hair, Killer used to mark the ball with classic Scanlens-footy-card timing. Josh Vansittart was in my year level and was my best mate; his dad, Roger, was a local policeman who had a fearsome reputation for having been an athletic, aggressive, bearded ruckman for Warragul in the 1970s. Legend had it that Roger was still serving a suspension from his last outing as a Warragul Gull. His son Josh might be the most physically courageous footballer I ever played with.

Reputations and myths are one thing, cold hard facts another. One of the boys playing in that car park was a lad named Damian Gargan. Like me, 'Gargs' was small, light and a bit timid, but his reputation was a little more elevated than the rest of us. Gargs's dad, Michael, had played three games for North Melbourne in the 1970s. I mean, he had actually played in the VFL! To me, Gargs may as well have been the son of Neil Armstrong. There was a book doing the rounds at the time that documented every single player to have ever played in the VFL/AFL. And there it was, in black ink: 'Michael Gargan, North Melbourne, 3 games'. I used to read that book and gawp. Imagine that.

3

I Met a Girl in High School

The world got a lot bigger in a very short time in 1995. It became an intoxicating mix of juvenile adventure, lunchtime football, and girls who all seemed to be wearing Impulse deodorant. I was a teenager, at last.

The previous year, my last at primary school, had felt claustrophobic. I was ready for some mischief and a new crowd. I'd done my time on the monkey bars at St Joe's, and I yearned for a bigger pond. I found it at Marist Sion.

A lot of kids feel a bit daunted about starting Year 7, because everything feels new, like being dropped in a foreign country. But because Mum had taught at the school for years and I had older siblings already well established there, I walked in with my shoulders down. I'd spent plenty of time there. I knew all the teachers. I wasn't going to get lost on the first day. I was ready. Come at me, world.

Mum wasn't just a teacher at Marist Sion, she was also the Year 7 coordinator. If school was a prison, Mum was the warden – at least to the first-year kids. So, I was 'connected'. Over the summer holidays, Mum had let me handpick my class. 7D was an all-star line-up of my best mates and the prettiest girls. I can see now that I was intoxicated by the power, and yes, it corrupted me.

I loved high school, I loved that there were all of these other kids from different towns that I didn't know. I had a healthy respect for my elders, but because I had a brother in Year 12 and a sister in Year 11, I never got hassled.

Football wasn't everything at Marist Sion, but it was the big show at lunchtime. We had some good footballers in my year level, but there were just as many if not more in the year above. At the start of Term 1 in 1995, the pecking order was sorting itself out and everyone was out to be the big fish. This pond had lots of different fish, all shapes and sizes, and suddenly I didn't feel like the big deal I'd thought I was in primary school anymore. This realisation was equal parts scary and exciting.

The lunchtime games of football that were played on the main oval featured some epic battles. It was a hybrid game, like a cross between footy and half-court basketball. One team would start by kicking the ball out from full-back, have to work it out to halfway, before turning around and attacking the goals.

It was a real treat to play on a proper oval during school hours. The loose gravel car park at St Joe's had lost its charm. This felt like a step into the big league. The ferocity of those lunchtime games was just as intense as any 'proper' game I played on the weekends for my home club, the Warragul Gulls Under 14s. It was great practice.

There was a big brother–little brother competitive thing going on between the Year 7 and Year 8 kids, and occasionally it would bubble into a fight where proper punches were thrown. But most of the time it was just hard, tough, fast footy. The stakes were high, but no-one was keeping score. What kept those competitive fires burning might have been the crowd we had drawn to watch us play. Girls. Lots of girls. This never happened at primary school.

Clustered around the oval, sitting on the low fence, were girls from Years 7, 8 and 9. With the benefit of hindsight, I now think most of them were probably there to perv on Simon Murnane. Tanned and muscled, with a shy smile that broke a few hearts, Murnane looked like Kelly Slater's son. The girls swooned every time he went near the footy.

Behind the goals at the western end of the oval was a row of tall pine trees that marked the school's border. It was also the site of many a first kiss. When there was a break in play or a hold-up to track down a match-standard footy, a prearranged romantic coupling might fill in the time. It was all very elaborate and the tension was exhilarating – not only for those taking part, but for the witnesses too. I was good at being a witness.

Everything was organised prior to the event by various messengers in the classrooms. Eventually one of the girls from the group on the sidelines would leave her post and walk towards the pines. The chosen boy would take her lead and follow her until the branches and leaves swallowed them up. After a few minutes, they'd emerge and return as heroes.

LEATHER SOUL

This courtship behaviour was quite formal and sincere in its privacy and ritualistic nature, but it wasn't without incident. One time, my mate Jake followed his girl, Erin, into the pines. As Jake returned to our group of boys and we set about starting up a game of footy, we heard loud shrieks of laughter from the girls huddled around Erin. All eyes turned to Jake; he just hung his head. It must not have gone well. Kissing was a skill that we would all have to master, and on that oval it was more valuable than precision kicking on your opposite foot.

My first kiss also happened in 1995 – at the Warragul show, behind the dodgem cars. I was going out with a girl called Liana. Ours was a controversial relationship, because she was in Year 8. It wasn't exactly the Montagues and the Capulets, but it did ruffle a few feathers. The Year 8 boys weren't too happy that I'd taken one

of their girls. The controversy should have centred around the fact that Liana was a foot taller than me and looked at least three years older, but that didn't seem to matter as we walked past the showbag stand holding hands.

I knew things were heating up when Liana led me away from the crowds and the bright lights. Sure enough, my first kiss followed and it was everything a first kiss should be. A bit awkward, a bit unreal. The fact that Liana had to lean down quite a way was the only imperfection. She was kind enough not to laugh about my technique or make fun of me to her friends, at least not while I was in earshot.

Liana and I were a sweet little couple, briefly. I would ring her and run through my limited list of conversation topics, and there were other kisses, but we didn't last long.

Truth be told, I was smitten with another girl. Her name was Justine Quigley.

I actually met Justine the year before, in 1994, at the Marist Sion Year 7 social. Because Mum was the Year 7 coordinator and I knew most of the kids, I didn't think it was weird at all that a Grade 6 kid like me would go along and get my boogie on with the high-school kids. Only one kid voiced their disapproval, and it was the girl of my dreams.

I fell in love with Justine the very first moment I saw her. It was a very *Wayne's World* 'Dream Weaver' kind of scene. I saw her and immediately felt something awaken in my soul. I knew this girl was different from the rest. She was so damn pretty, and didn't look or carry herself like anyone else I'd ever met. And she was a bit mean to me. Does it get much better than that?

I took my seat next her on the plastic classroom chairs that lined the walls around the dance floor, while 'Waterfalls' by TLC blared out of the speakers. I turned to her, she moved her head sideways towards me, and time stood still.

Then she bluntly asked, 'What are you even doing here?'

I couldn't come up with an answer and the meeting was over, washed away in a stream of kids and pop music. Rattled but not defeated, I just stared at her from afar for the rest of the evening. When she snuck off to kiss Tim McMahon behind the quadrangle, I went with my mate Paul to see if we could get a glimpse. From the shadows, we watched their silhouettes melt into each other. I don't know if I did this for a cheap thrill or as part of some emotional self-harming exercise. Everything about it was regrettable.

Things went much better once I arrived at Marist Sion in a more official capacity. Every time I saw Justine in the schoolyard I was hypnotised by her. It wasn't just a teenage hormonal thing (although there was obviously a bit of that there too). Something else was going on.

Justine's best friend was a girl I'd known for years, Lauren Galloway, and together Justine and Lauren used to get up to all kinds of mischief. One day when I bumped into them at school, they were drinking tequila from a drink bottle. They were laughing, teasing, swaying and shooting off mysterious looks in my direction. This kind of thing didn't happen at St Joe's. I was worried about

Justine getting sick from the booze or in trouble if she got caught by the teachers, but I was also attracted to the danger of it too.

I had a bowl-cut hairdo, Richmond Tigers boxer shorts under my school shorts, my shirt was tucked in and I had once had a sip of Dad's wine. Rock'n'roll. Justine had a small, tight ponytail with red dye through it, the shortest school dress in the history of short school dresses, and she was drunk at midday on a school day. Blimey! Life was picking up pace. I was a little kid and Justine's rebellious streak left me in the dust, but she gave me a bit of time at recess and lunchtimes. Something was happening. Change was on the way.

A few weeks after Tequila Tuesday, the school had its annual swimming sports. I wasn't the strongest swimmer and I wasn't jumping out of my pale skin and skinny body to stand on the starter's blocks. I sat next to Justine for most of the day, and it was one of the greatest days of my life. With all the colour, energy, chanting and cheering going on around us, we just sat on the grass and talked about stuff. About boys, girls and school. Sweet, innocent stuff. Then she told me about how her dad had died four years earlier in a car accident. But she only hinted at the damage, confusion and trauma in her heart. There was an ocean of anger, pain and sadness in her eyes. I wanted to hold her, kiss her, make her feel safe. Instead, I just sat there, tearing away little pieces of grass from the patch in front of us.

Occasionally I had to go and compete in an event, but I was much faster getting back to that bit of lawn next to my girl than I was through the water.

That hot summer day felt like it went on forever, but eventually the carnival wound up and the sea of kids headed for the buses out the front. I walked home. Even then, I think I knew instinctively that life would be different tomorrow. Justine had let me into her world like she'd let no-one else in. At least, that's what it felt like. We weren't a couple, but it was a connection that I can only describe as spiritual. I was hers forever and she was mine. This was beyond the pine trees. For the rest of the year we would write each other little letters that were romantic in their innocence and pass them back and forth. There is nothing on this earth that has come close to the excitement of Justine pressing a letter into my palm as we crossed paths with one another in the schoolyard.

All of that alone would have made 1995 special, but there were other narratives running alongside the fun and games of high school. One of those was the resurgent Richmond Tigers. Up until this point of my life, there hadn't been much to cheer about if you were a Tigers supporter, but all that changed in one glorious football season. Something had been brewing: the year before, a young colt from Devonport, Tasmania, had burst onto the AFL scene with high marking, long runs up and down the ground and some erratic kicking and behaviour that demanded your attention. Matthew 'Richo' Richardson had arrived, and suddenly people were talking about the Tigers.

Our family jumped on the bandwagon, and we spent most weekends driving down to the MCG to watch the Tigers play emotion-charged football that moved with a heaving momentum.

For years, our family's AFL appetite had usually only taken us as far as Waverley Park, which was about 45 minutes from Warragul, but Dad picked up on our level of excitement and the potential of John Northey's boys. I always loved my footy, but the excitement that ran up my legs as Dad parked the car in the back streets of Richmond and we joined the yellow and black march towards the MCG was something else.

It's such a Melbourne experience to put your team's scarf around your neck on a chilly Friday night and head towards the bright lights of the hallowed MCG. It never gets old, but in 1995 it felt new to me. The communal excitement of being among the Tiger army, making our way to worship not just Richo, but Brodders, Benny, Scotty Turner, Knighter, Freeza and Cambo, as well had us all buzzing. With Wayne Campbell's 9 on my back I would watch him closely and feel good every time he got a kick, which was often. But there was nothing quite like the exhilaration of seeing number 12 in full flight. No-one in the league played like Richo, and in '95 he was at his breathtaking best.

We always sat behind the goals in the Ponsford Stand. Walking to the stadium, Dad, for some reason, would walk 20 or 30 metres in front of us, which used to infuriate Mum because it meant we were all gasping for breath to catch up. Once we'd taken our seats, Dad would go to work with the *Footy Record*, filling in the goals and points for no-one in particular. Occasionally he'd yell out, 'They don't want it!' if the Tigers laid a succession of tackles and the opposition coughed the ball up. My brother would sit next to me, but we watched the game differently. Ben would sit forward, trying to get some sense of the tactics and patterns used by the coaches and their players. I'd follow the ball and make notes to myself about which players made good decisions when they got the ball. Mum would take until quarter-time to forgive Dad for walking ahead of us again.

The Tigers won the first nine games of the '95 season, and Monday mornings at school were suddenly glorious. It was all going so well – until Richo went down clutching his knee at the SCG. He was out for the year. It was such a cruel blow.

That didn't stop the Tigers charging towards their first finals appearance since 1982. The semi-final against the Bombers, when we came back from five goals down to win, remains to this day one of my best days in footy. The heroics of Matthew Knight's three first-half goals, the brute physicality of Scotty Turner, along with the efforts of every player in yellow and black, left a big impression on me. We smiled all the way home to Warragul, our Tigers scarves hanging out the window, flapping proudly in the wind. We got belted by the Cats in the preliminary final the next week, but that didn't really matter. The sun had come out for us Tigers supporters and we'd be better next year, surely. I set about making plans to one day play for the Tigers, but in the meantime I had to grow my hair long so I could look like Richo, Benny, Cambo and Bondy. 'For we're from Ti-ger, Yellow and Black!'

Ah 1995, one of the best years ever.

Wednesday, 15 October 2014: Peter Gordon's place

There's business to attend to on my walk with Peter Gordon today: the captaincy of the Bulldogs. I desperately want to be captain, but more than that, I want Peter to want me to be captain. He has invited to his house to go for a walk and I assume he is going to offer me the role. I hope I'm right.

Peter appears at his door dressed in long shorts and a flat-peak cap. He has just returned home from a holiday in New York. With all the drama that's erupted off the field since the siren sounded on the Bulldogs' disastrous 2014 season, we have a lot to talk about.

Peter and I haven't spent huge chunks of time together, and this is our first walk, but I've always felt we shared a fondness for one another. I first heard Peter talk publicly at his induction into the Western Bulldogs Hall of Fame in 2010. I instantly warmed to his passionate and emotional memories and stories. I mean, he was the guy who saved our club back in 1989. I thought of him as a football romantic like me.

But today is not a nostalgic walk down memory lane. It's more of a military-style update and call to arms. The conversation flows quickly, matching the tempo of our stride along the riverside trail. I ask some questions, but mainly listen as Peter fills me in on the details of the departure of our captain, Ryan Griffen, to the GWS Giants; the termination of coach Brendan McCartney's contract;

and the recruitment of Tom Boyd from GWS. Since it's the off-season, all the information I've had about these events until now has been through the newspapers. It's comforting to hear the details behind the headlines from Peter.

We're about half an hour into our walk when I sense the conversation is leading to the crucial point. Sure enough, Peter asks me, 'Why haven't you been considered for the captaincy before?'

It's a fair question. I tell him that contrary to some reports, I've never coveted the job. For a long time, I wouldn't have been a good captain, and when I reached the point where maybe I could have been considered, I always thought there was someone better for the job. Perhaps I lacked the courage to put my name up for it in case I missed out. When players were jockeying to take Brad Johnson's place after he stood down as skipper in 2010, I stood back. I didn't get the sense from Rocket Eade, our coach at the time, that I was his kind of candidate as a captain, and I was so consumed with getting my body right that I was perhaps not selfish, but certainly self-absorbed. It's pretty hard for people to see you as a leader if you don't see yourself in that light. When the captaincy went from Matty Boyd to Ryan Griffen, I was fully supportive and saw my role as being the same as it had been for years – to be a confidante for the skipper.

Peter and I keep stride in silence for a few moments before I finish saying my piece. 'But I want to be captain now and I know I'm the right person for the job. I hope that fits with what the club wants.' The words come out just as I'd rehearsed them in the car an hour earlier.

Peter seems relieved and maybe even excited that I want the job. He shares with me that it is also the wish of the board that I be appointed skipper after the right process has taken place.

I'm lost in listening to Peter's updates on my new and departing teammates and the challenges this will pose for the incoming skipper when I look down and notice something spray-painted, in wonky, faded black capitals, on the footbridge we're crossing. Peter hasn't seen it and has walked on ahead without me. I have to call him back. We stand side by side, looking down at the word on the concrete footbridge, as the Yarra River flows beneath us.

CAPTAIN

It's a surreal moment. Why was that word there, at that exact moment?

Peter and I keep walking, although our pace slows a bit now that the business has been attended to. With the rhythm of our feet I think we both signed an agreement of sorts: to stick together and navigate a difficult time for the club. We have each other's backs.

It feels good. I feel exhilarated, to be honest. At 32, and with 250 games under my belt, I suddenly feel like I am at the start of a new adventure, not managing the death of a career.

Oh, and we have a new coach too – Peter tells me that yesterday he offered the job to Luke Beveridge.

Our walk is done. The wide, open road ahead has just come into view.

4

Football's Chook Raffle

I managed to navigate my junior football career through those difficult puberty years and continued to build a reputation at school and in the local football leagues as a player to watch. The trophy cabinet was fully stacked. I was rail thin, but I was fast, could read the game and could kick with both feet. I followed the traditional path of inter-league teams and junior schoolboy selections. But when I became eligible for the Gippsland Power Under 18s training squad, I was left out. I was furious. I couldn't believe it. Half a dozen boys from my school had been invited to join the squad and I thought I was better than all of them. It lit a fire in me. After a month or so, I was given a late invite and I made it onto the list and into the team for the start of the season. I really wanted it now and trained harder than I ever had. The bitter jealousy and disappointment stayed with me and gave me a new sense of determination. I found out later that it was a very deliberate ploy by the coach of the Power, Peter Francis, to delay my inclusion. Peter knew I could play, he'd watched me dominate school football as a 12-year-old, but he also knew that the game had always come too easy for me and that my laid-back attitude might be the thing that would hold me back from becoming a league footballer one day. I often wonder what would have happened to me if Peter had just picked me on natural talent. That's more than just good coaching.

Midway through 1999, my Year 11, a letter with maroon and blue letterhead arrived at our Warragul home. It was from the Brisbane Lions Football Club. The letter was straightforward: it encouraged me to nominate for the upcoming AFL draft.

God only knows how many similar letters were sent out all over the land, but at 186 Albert Road it was like Charlie Bucket had just found the golden ticket. We held that letter aloft in the lounge room and whooped in triumph. I had been a good junior footballer, but this was the most encouraging sign yet that I might actually become an AFL player. These were heady times.

As a bottom-age 17-year-old for the Gippsland Power Under 18s, I had started slowly, but improved as the season went on. By the end of the season, I was one of the team's best players. All of a sudden, my name was being thrown around in AFL recruiting circles and potential clubs and managers started visiting our home. It was thrilling for the whole family. The only sour note was one night when I was at a mate's house after school playing *Super Mario Kart* on the Nintendo and the phone rang. It was Mum, and she needed to speak with me right away. 'Get home now – John Hook from the Hawthorn Football Club is in the lounge room, and you're supposed to be here!' I'd mixed up the times of the appointment. Even as a carefree 17-year-old, I knew this wasn't good.

I rode my bike home as fast as I could and put on my best 'I'm ready for the challenge, sir!' face. But it didn't stop Mr Hook reminding my parents and I about my little mix-up on three separate occasions during that first meeting. I'm not sure if that cooled the interest from Glenferrie, but we didn't hear from them after that. Oh well, I never did like the Hawks.

For a little while it seemed like I might be getting picked up by the West Coast Eagles, which had Mum a little flustered. Perth was such a long way away. As the draft drew closer, it became apparent that I wasn't a draft smoky, but a virtual certainty. It was a strange year: life just kept picking up pace, quicker and quicker, as unstoppable as a big steam engine.

By the end of the season with Gippsland Power, I was being handed the big jobs on bigger opponents. My best performances came in the finals series, when all the recruiters were there with their clipboards and suspicious eyes. Gippsland Power went all the way to Grand Final Day at the MCG, only to go down to the Sandringham Dragons.

I felt right at home on the big stage. We played the curtain raiser to the reserves, who were playing before the Kangaroos took on Carlton for the AFL premiership. The game kicked off at breakfast time, about 9 am. But that didn't matter. The MCG is just as glorious with nine spectators as 90,000. The grass was immaculate, like carpet, and the speed of the game was quicker than I'd ever played before. We were beaten convincingly, but that childhood spark lit up like a flame. I'm going to be a league player one day. It was really happening.

A few weeks later, on the morning of the draft, there was an article in the paper predicting the top ten players. I was gobsmacked to see my name and picture at number 10. An unnamed recruiter described me as 'skinny as skinny'.

I didn't mind where I went, but staying in Victoria had more appeal for obvious reasons. The Eagles had picks 11 and 14. Wedged in between them, at pick 13, were the Western Bulldogs, who were apparently keen but had been very secretive. The only time I had spoken with anyone from the club was at the draft camp in Canberra. Scotty Clayton was the recruiting manager, and he had whisked me away from prying eyes for a chat behind the basketball courts. It was a short conversation in comparison to the ones I'd had with other clubs, all of which were held out in the open. There was a clandestine vibe. At one stage Scotty asked me how tall my parents were. I may have given them both an extra inch or two.

The Eagles took Darren Glass at pick 11, Port Adelaide chose Paul Koulouriotis at 12, and then my moment arrived. 'Pick 13, Western Bulldogs … Robert Murphy, Gippsland Power.'

Pandemonium broke out in the Murphy household. The steam train reached for a higher gear. I was quickly on the phone talking to the coach, Terry Wallace. He congratulated me, then said, 'The hard work starts now.'

Justine was also at our house that day. By now, our relationship had fallen into a very unusual normality. We weren't a couple – in fact, I think she may have had a boyfriend at the time – but we were *something*. In a room full of people, we always kept an eye on each other. With hindsight, I think both of us assumed that one day we would end up together, but there was a bit of unspoken restlessness. Neither of us was willing to put our true feelings right out there. But Justine says that the day I was drafted she felt a little sad, as if her 'Robbie' was being taken away.

People from all over town came to our home to join the party, and there were moments of poignancy among the delirium. Our neighbour Connie Matthews came over and put her arms around me. She had tears streaming down her face. Her husband, Bob, had played reserves football for Footscray back in the day and been a barber in Seddon for many years. Bob had been like a surrogate grandfather to me. He'd recently passed away. The only time Bob ever got cross with me was when I trampled over his front garden fetching my tattered footy. He was a gentle man with a knack for a yarn. Connie is with Bob now. They were beautiful people. Maybe it's because I was the baby in our family, but I always had a deep respect for my elders.

Despite the heartfelt moment with Connie, I did lose a bit of perspective on draft day, but in the best way possible. I mean, one day you're collecting footy cards, and the next day you're on a footy card! It doesn't get much better than that, at least not in my 17-year-old world. It was a lot to take in. I don't regret getting carried away. I've always been offended by any sense of nonchalance from a new draftee in the years since. Don't be mature or professional about it, kid. Get excited!

In the days after the draft, Mum and I went down to the local video store and rented the documentary *Year of the Dogs*. Later, when I mentioned this story to some people at the Bulldogs, they shuddered and looked away. In some ways, the film didn't exactly show the club in its best light, but that's not how the Murphys looked at it. We saw a club – a real, bona fide footy club – that had heart and spirit.

A week later, the club welcomed all of the draftees down to the Kennel, Whitten Oval, to meet everyone and watch the team train. There was quite a big litter of pups that year. The tour of the club with our parents, meeting coaches and players, felt like an out-of-body experience. 'That's Chris Grant over there. Oh look – Nathan Brown, the young, cocky prodigy, is coming over to shake my hand.' My whole body tingled with excitement, and then they gave us a bag full of tracksuits, training tops, runners and shorts. It was better than my best-ever Christmas morning.

Everyone was ushered upstairs to the social club, where president David Smorgon addressed the club and unofficially opened the 2000 pre-season. I sat behind Kingsley Hunter and Steven Kretiuk and strained to hear their conversation. I heard the recent footy trip mentioned, followed by some laughter, and then something about Nicky Winmar, or 'Cuz' as they called him. Drama was unfolding apparently, but what exactly was a mystery to me.

Two of us pups – Daniel Giansiracusa and I – weren't allowed to train for another couple of weeks because we were too young. I was shattered that I couldn't go out onto the training track with the whole group as everyone dispersed from the social club rooms. Gia and I watched on with our parents and football manager Paul Armstrong from high up in the stands. My enthusiasm for training began to fade when I saw what they were doing – repeated one-kilometre time trials on a soft deck. It looked torturous, and a few of our fellow draftees seemed to be having a tough time of it. I'm not sure how Gia felt, but I was nervous. We'd get our turn soon enough.

The Murphys drove back down the highway under grey skies, but I was full of sunshine, cloaked in a new reality and a brand-new Western Bulldogs tracksuit. As we rolled past Pakenham, the news came over the car radio: 'Nicky Winmar did not show for day one of pre-season at the Western Bulldogs, and it is believed he will retire from the game.' It was the only sour note on a sweet, sweet day.

*

I had two weeks to pack up my life with Mum and Dad in Warragul. I was leaving home for good, and I felt ready. Of course, in hindsight, I wasn't. Mum has since told me she had a hard time letting me, the last of her kids to leave home, go, but I didn't notice. My head was up in the clouds. Let's not forget: I was on a footy card.

Justine had left town too. She was heading north with her boyfriend to live in sunny Queensland. Just before she left we had a fight. She told me she was going and I didn't say much. Maybe I should have told her to stay. Maybe that's why we had a fight.

Warragul is only 75 minutes away from Melbourne. At first, I moved into my sister's flat in North Melbourne. Bridget was studying sport and recreation at Victoria University in Footscray. I slept on a mattress in her lounge room. It wasn't glamorous, but I didn't care. I had my bag full of fresh Bulldogs apparel and I felt ready for my football adventure.

The Bulldogs' welfare manager, Gary McGorlick (better known as Brutus), had arranged for one of the senior players to pick me up for training each day. I was eight months short of being eligible to get my driver's licence. Ruckman Luke Darcy was my new chauffeur, and I was pumped. I'd seen him on television. He was a good player – a really good player, actually.

Every day, Darce would pick me up; we'd chat for a while until the conversation dried up and Luke would turn the volume up on the stereo. Invariably, something from the Red Hot Chilli Peppers' album *Californication* was playing. When I hear songs from that album now, I smile; it takes me back to the start of a long friendship founded on that commute to Footscray.

One day, I waited out the front of my sister's flat and no-one arrived. I had a problem. We had a running session scheduled at Newport athletics track, and I was going to be late. I didn't want to cause a fuss by ringing Luke, so I ran back inside to Bridget. I'd only been training for a couple of weeks, but I already knew that being late for training was very serious. There could be consequences, even for a rookie.

'Where do you need to go?' Bridget asked.

'Newport athletics track,' I replied.

'Where's that?'

'I dunno actually ... but it's got a really tall chimney or pylon nearby.'

'Right,' came the slightly exasperated reply.

We jumped in her olive-green Gemini and headed west. Once we were over the Maribyrnong, the chimney tower I'd remembered came into view and like an old sailboat captain might use the moon and stars to find his way home, we set out in its direction. My eyes darted from the clock on the dashboard to the skyline, back and forth like a vertical tennis match. With some nifty driving, Bridget pulled into the car park and I could see the swarm of tall men in blue singlets drifting slowly across to the dreaded red rubber surface of the running track. I might make it!

I jumped out, yelled 'Thank you!' over my shoulder, and was absorbed into the deep blue singlet sea. No-one batted an eyelid. Nice one, Sis.

I never did find out why Luke forgot me that day. Maybe I'd worn him out with all of my questions.

*

Training to play AFL isn't actually that glamorous today, and it was even less glamorous in 1999, but I loved it all the same. I was so young, so naive, but I was doing it. I had a football club and I really wanted to stay there for as long as I could. Everyone's first pre-season is a shock to the system. Mine was no different. I don't care how hard you thought you trained before you arrived, pre-season is a whole new level. All you do is train, eat large meals and sleep at any opportunity.

I grew to love pre-seasons, but my first couple were scary. The fear came from a lack of confidence. 'Will I make it through the session?' Fatigue partnered with that kind of anxiety fills each lap of the field with dread. At times, every single step felt painful. As a new recruit, your resistance to pain just isn't there yet, and your will to push through is no stronger than a tissue.

I remember with a twinge a particularly torrid handball game, when I was so tired that I missed a series of simple handballs, giving the ball back to the other team. One of the other players said, loud enough for me to hear, 'You're a fuckin' spastic, Murph.' I was crushed. I knew that I wasn't yet a part of the team. I had to keep my head down. This was a very combative era, when punches were quite regularly thrown during training sessions. And I was just a kid. During that first pre-season, I remember not having underarm hair; I would avoid any warm-up stretches that exposed this. It took a couple of years for my fitness to build and my body to develop.

One of the peculiarities of that first year was that I still had to finish my schooling. My first year in Melbourne was split between Whitten Oval and Year 12 at Footscray City College. I'd left any scholastic ambitions behind years ago. I was a footy player. I embarked on a Year 12 curriculum that screamed 'bare minimum': four subjects, when nearly everyone else did five. I wouldn't get a score, but I would pass. I can't imagine Mum and Dad were over the moon about this, but my decline in output at school had been steady for a few years. It was no secret. My folks let me find my own path, even if it was unorthodox. The main challenge was keeping my attendance above the required 80 per cent – difficult with my training commitments and no car.

By the time the school year rolled around, I was living with my brother in a unit on Somerville Road in Kingsville. I needed a more permanent living arrangement and Ben needed a flatmate. I remember, with a cold shiver up my spine, the weekly Tuesday night depression as I contemplated my Wednesday schedule. Here's how it ran:

6 – 7.30 am: Weights at the club

9 am – 3.30 pm: Full day of school classes (no free periods)

4.15 pm: Picked up by teammate Simon Atkins for training at Werribee (the Bulldogs' VFL affiliate)

9.30 pm: Home

After the morning weights session, I'd sometimes hop into the spa at the club, wedge my head in the corner, and go back to sleep. When I woke up, fingers like sultanas, I'd trudge off to collect my bike and ride to school.

Those early days were tough, but the thought of giving up never entered my mind. I was quietly determined to stick it out and make something of myself.

And by the middle of that first year, things were on the up. Under Alastair Clarkson at Werribee I started to string together some good games and was named emergency for the senior team eight weeks in a row. Alastair would go on to be the greatest coach of the modern era. He was very gentle with me in my first year of playing football against men.

Eventually I made my debut, against Carlton at Princes Park on 15 July 2000. It was like stepping into the television screen at Mum and Dad's house. At one point during the game a melee broke out. It moved around me like I was a rock in a stream. I was politely ignored by the 'real men'. I remember seeing Tony Liberatore lunging at Aaron Hamill, grabbing a piece of his jumper and screaming, 'You and me! You and fucking me!' Hamill seemed half man, half gorilla. He was fearsome. He looked like he wanted to kill Libba. Players from all around dragged them away from each other. Toto, I thought to myself, this ain't Kansas!

I played quite well that day: kicked a goal late in the game to put us in front, and played keepings off in the dying seconds to hold off the Blues for a memorable win. I felt composed out there. When the siren sounded, Simon Garlick grabbed me in a headlock and growled, 'Where have you been all year?' Garlo kicked six goals that day. I felt part of the team from that moment on.

The first three games of my AFL career would be the envy of most footballers. In that first one, we were rank underdogs and beat Carlton by three points. The next week we beat Collingwood by nine points at the Docklands, and I managed to keep my spot despite not touching the ball. In game number three, we were to play Essendon on Friday night. Match of the round against the unbeaten

Bombers. They'd won 20 games in a row. It was unheard of.

In the build-up that week, our coach, Terry 'Plough' Wallace, came up with an extreme game plan. Internally, it was dubbed 'the super flood'. It was the kind of tactic that needed a charismatic frontman, and Plough could certainly charm a group if he was in the mood. We would play 14 players in the back half of the ground, where there's usually six. This kind of thing was radical. It's just as radical now as it was then. I knew this was going to cause a big fuss, whatever the result. I went to school that Friday tingling. I had a big secret in my pocket.

Footscray City College was a wild mix of kids from all origins and ethnic backgrounds. It wasn't a footy-mad school like the one I was used to in Warragul, but there was still a bunch of kids at Footscray who were into it and wanted to know all about that night's big game. I kept the super flood to myself.

That night, the Bulldogs got up by 11 points, ending Essendon's historic winning streak. Dramatically, Chris Grant kicked a left-foot snap from the boundary to put us in front in the dying minutes. There was a big brawl at half-time. This game had it all. The super flood was the talk of the town. It remains one of the most unusual games of football ever played. I barely rate a mention in it, although I did touch the ball.

I was dropped the week after, but to be honest I didn't really care. I was now officially an AFL player. My name was in the book, just down the alphabetical line from Mick Gargan. There it was in black and white. 'Robert Murphy. Western Bulldogs.

LEATHER SOUL

3 games.' And by now I had my licence and a car. A white Holden Barina with an alpine sticker down the side door. Form an orderly queue, ladies.

*

I was satisfied with my first year in the game, but as every young player finds out, you have to keep backing it up, week after week, year after year. The unrelenting forward momentum of progress in football is ever present. When pre-season number two was in full swing I was more curious about the world around me. I started to explore different parts of Melbourne in my downtime. I didn't have school to worry about. I had passed Year 12! I made those kind-hearted teachers work hard to get me there, I can tell you. I didn't even get close to 80 per cent attendance, but with some creative accounting and a few extensions here and there, we did it.

With my new level of freedom and having been accepted as part of the playing group, it was time to have some fun. I'll never forget the day Nathan Brown took me out for a beer in Fitzroy and we wandered into the Napier Hotel. We sat at the bar sipping pots of Carlton Draught. Nathan flirted with one of the barmaids, but I was distracted by the music coming out of the speakers.

'Who are we listening to?' I asked.

'The Rolling Stones,' came the reply.

'Oh yeah, which album?'

'*Exile on Main St.*'

How many moments can you remember when your life took a left turn? This was one of those. The music, the bar, the grungy clientele: they all collided. I wanted to be in this scene. I never did go to university, but after that day I began my own private degree in the history of rock'n'roll. It's been a lifelong quest. I was hooked. *Exile* remains my all-time favourite album.

When training resumed, expectations had gone up. I was a second-year player now, so I had to improve: the microscope was on me. My coaches were noticeably harder on me than they'd been in my first year. One of them was David Noble, who was head of development. Nobes is a shrewd operator. He's smart and has gone on to create an impressive football CV at several clubs. During this pre-season, though, I thought he was a total prick.

He was hard on the young players, and that's fair enough, but I felt like it went a bit far; he would never dare speak to the senior players the way he spoke to us. On one hot day during the summer of 2001 we were in the midst of two-on-one competitive work in a confined space. It's about as hard as training gets. It's hell. I was hunched over the ball, getting buffeted around by much bigger men, and all I could hear in the distance was Nobes and that distinctive, sarcastic tone in his voice.

'Come on, Murph … Oh come on, Murph!'

I snapped. 'Fuck off, Nobes.'

It wasn't loud, but it was loud enough for him to hear something. His head cocked. 'What was that?'

In for a penny, in for a pound. I spat back, 'Get fucked.'

This time he heard exactly what I'd said, and so did a few of the senior players, who let out that 'oh boy' groan. The drill was stopped and Nobes was understandably livid. I think I heard Nobes swear under his breath. I'd really upset him. Training moved on and we went to our separate corners. Jose Romero took me for a walk and talk. He put his arm around me. By this stage I'd cooled down and was mortified by my brief but brattish outburst.

Jose spoke softly. 'You know he can be a prick, I know he can be a prick, but you just can't say that, son.'

He wasn't renowned for his tender touch, Jose, but he showed me a gentle elder's care that day. I still feel a deep loyalty to him because of that one conversation. I don't think my relationship with Nobes ever fully recovered and I have to live with that. He was hard on me, but I needed that.

Tuesday, 24 February 2015: Whitten Oval, training session

The timing has worked out better than I could have hoped for. Our first NAB Cup game of the new season and my first as skipper is going to be against the Tigers at our spiritual home, the Whitten Oval. Our main training session for the week is scheduled for this afternoon. With an upcoming game back at the Whitten Oval this weekend, it's the perfect time for Wheels to address the team.

Back in 2003, the club arranged for Bulldogs legend Terry Wheeler to speak to the players about what it means to pull on the club jumper and play for the Bulldogs. At the time, we were a young team that was down near the bottom of the ladder, looking to crawl our way up. Wheels' talk to the club was the greatest footy speech I've ever heard. His words left a mark on me like a meteorite that's crashed to earth. He didn't just talk about the footy club, but about Footscray as a suburb and how the football club is woven into this place in the west of Melbourne, with its working-class roots. Essentially, he explained why we are the way we are. We're outsiders. I soaked it up like a sponge.

For the last couple of seasons, I've dreamt of getting Wheels back to the club to give that speech again. So when I became captain a few months ago, I wrote 'Terry Wheeler' in my tattered notebook and underlined it. As their leader, I want to bring education through storytelling back to the playing group. It's become a lost art in football clubs.

I liked Brendan McCartney, our coach from 2011 to 2014 – he had a traditional vision of how a club should operate and the importance of each person's role in that club being valued, from the boot studder right up to the president. He was almost manic in his insistence on 'team first' over the individual. I always admired that, and his work ethic. It was routine for Macca to visit injured players in hospital. Some people don't think that takes much effort, but I do. Unfortunately, in his last year, everything unravelled.

One criticism I do have of our former coach, though, was his inability to articulate what our story was. Who were we? At times, I felt like we were chasing a ghost. With Macca having shaped the Geelong powerhouse teams of the late 2000s, it's understandable that he would be heavily influenced by his own experiences. But I felt at times our team lacked an identity of our own. Some people pass this off as doe-eyed romance, but in among the marks, kicks, handballs, hard-ball gets, process and structure lie the intangibles of football. Identity is one of those, and it's a blood relative of traditional values like guts and spirit. Without the raw playing talent of the premiership Cats, I felt as if the best we could ever aspire to be was a watered-down version of a team from five years ago. A kind of 'Diet Geelong'.

The most exciting times I've had in football have been when I was part of a team that felt unique. Whether it's a placebo or an etched-in-stone fact, really believing that who you are and what you're doing sets you apart from your opposition is a powerful force in team sport. I want to help bring that feeling back to the Bulldogs this year, and when I asked our new coach, Luke Beveridge, if he was okay with me bringing Wheels in, he seemed into the idea.

So now here we are, walking straight off the training track in our boots and sweaty jumpers and filing into the theatrette. Most of the players have no idea what we've got planned.

I stand up in front of the players and staff to introduce Wheels, and I feel like a captain. You can compare captaincy to fatherhood in some ways. A lot of the time you just feel like a bloke with kids, and then something happens. Like carrying one of your children into the house from the car when they've fallen asleep after a long trip. In those moments, you're really a dad. It's the same with the captaincy. Most of the time you're just one of the boys, and then there's a moment that makes you feel you are truly the captain. Their captain.

I take a couple of minutes to introduce Wheels, because I assume a lot of the younger boys don't know who he is or fully appreciate his place in our club's history. Terry Wheeler is the greatest football orator I've ever heard, and I've listened to plenty.

Wheels takes the podium and begins speaking about the significance of the muddy banks along the Maribyrnong, where men worked as blacksmiths, slaughtermen and the like. He paints a rich picture of a blue-collar suburb steeped in hard, honest work. He talks about players who've worn our jumper and how, while their day is long passed, if you ask them they will still tell you passionately, 'This is my club!' He reels off half a dozen names, finishing with 'Robert "Bones" McGhie – he'll tell you, this is my club!'

Bones played at a few clubs, so to hear that he too thought of the Bulldogs in this way emphasises the point wonderfully.

Wheels' passion and eloquence are just as I remembered from 12 years ago, but I am sitting up the front and can't tell what the young guys behind me are thinking. Wheels powers on, turning towards our ground, the Whitten Oval. He touches on the fact that we are coming home, and describes what it's like to play in front of our mob, the exhilaration of winning in front of them. 'The ground, the dirt, mud, wind, rain and grass – it's our spiritual home.' It is an emphatic note to finish on.

The room is quiet, but in a good way. I thank Wheels for his time, and I am encouraged that most of the players shake his hand on their way out. I think the talk has hit the right note. But it's not until the players are congregating in the locker room that my concerns are fully eased. They loved it. There's even a bit of talk among a few of the younger players about wanting to play right then and there. I know that feeling.

With some history in our bellies, it's time to explore the hunger in our hearts. To start writing our own story and see where it takes us.

5

Conscripts and Volunteers

I copped a few verbal sprays along the football trail. If I'm being honest, I was the kind of young player who needed a spray every so often. I was a bit of a floater, lacking intensity and prone to bouts of daydreaming. One day I was up for the fight, the next I wasn't.

One particular dressing down stands head and shoulders above all the others. It's the one that gets brought up at boozy lunches with old teammates. It's funny. I even revel in retelling it over a cold beer. But at the time, I thought my soul would melt into the carpet of the Princes Park change rooms.

It was 2001 and my career was in its infancy; I'd barely played ten games. We'd just been handed a drubbing by the Blues. The sun was setting on the Terry Wallace–era Bulldogs team; there would be no more finals for this stoic bunch of old veterans and crop of pups who weren't yet ready for the weekly grind. On this day, I felt all at sea, but I wasn't alone. It was a dirty day for the Dogs.

As we entered the locker room, we could still hear the Carlton theme song being blasted out across the ground and the Blues' supporters singing loudly. All that was waiting for us was a row of stony faces. 'Straight into the meeting room.' Gulp.

Two headings were written on the whiteboard, with players' names evenly placed under them. One column was headed 'Volunteers', the other was 'Conscripts'.

It's amazing how quickly you can find your own name in such situations. There was mine, down the bottom of a long list under 'Conscripts'. My initial reaction was relief. I didn't really know what the word 'conscript' meant – I'd never heard it in any context before – but my gut feeling was that it sounded better than 'volunteer'. More sophisticated somehow. It was only after scanning the other names in my list that a sense of unease started to rise in my chest.

Like the team mascot, I was sitting cross-legged at the front of the group. This was also a mistake – I was only two feet away from a seething Terry Wallace.

Then Plough started up. Two things became very clear from the start: this was not going to be your average post-match debrief; and it was much better to be a Volunteer than a Conscript.

The theme of the review was war and which of our soldiers had retained some honour in defeat. There were quite a few names under the 'Volunteer' banner and Plough heaped praise on them. I was only half listening, as I was preparing myself for what was about to come my way, but I do recall at one point Plough describing Luke Darcy as a colonel. Darcy had been 'tough, bold and brave in the face of the enemy'. I'd have cut off my arm right then and there to be thought of in that light. But I was a Conscript, whatever that meant.

After addressing the volunteers, Plough turned his attention to the rest of us. The tone of his voice changed, along with his body language. So did the mood in the tiny, jam-packed meeting room. Plough started stalking the room, walking back and forth as he shot out verbal barb after barb to a group he said 'didn't come prepared for war'.

Rohan Smith was singled out for 'being beaten by a better prepared warrior' (the Blues' Simon Beaumont). Kingsley Hunter was pronounced M.I.A. 'Kinger – you're still over there! We had to retreat and fly the choppers out and we couldn't find you! Who fucken' knows where you are?!' Then it was Nathan Eagleton's turn. 'Eags' had kicked a goal late in the game long after the result had been decided, and had a pretty quiet day before that. 'Eags! You only started shooting when the war was over! Everyone had started walking home and only then did you stand up and start shooting the enemy in the back!'

Around this time, something peculiar started happening in that tiny meeting room. One of Plough's assistant coaches, Phil Maylin, was standing stage left and caught my eye. His head was down and his eyes were fixed to the floor, but I could sense that he was having trouble keeping his composure. Little fits of laughter were bubbling up inside him. I'm only giving you the greatest hits of this 'spray': by this stage it had been going for 15 or 20 minutes. There was a sense of the ridiculousness about the whole thing.

Then came my turn. 'Murph, you were disgraceful! This war was fought toe-to-toe! Hand-to-hand combat! The enemy grabbed your own fucking knife out of your hands and stabbed you with it! BANG! YOU'RE DEAD!'

Adding to the drama of the moment was the fact that I was sitting on the floor just under Plough, so when he described my demise he was in a position to actually act out what happened. When it came to the big crescendo – 'BANG! YOU'RE DEAD!' – Plough actually stabbed me with an imaginary blade. Phil Maylin was now visibly shaking with giggles.

It may have been funny to Maylin, but to me, as a new recruit, it was anything but. It was a humiliating experience, but it was typical of the time. I didn't feel victimised or unfairly treated: the coach's word was gospel.

That night we had the mid-year ball for the whole football club. Isn't it always the way that when a football function is booked in advance, the side gets belted on the same day? I went along, but inside I felt a deep sense of shame and embarrassment. In the movie *Saving Private Ryan* there's a scene where a soldier has his own knife turned on him by a German soldier. Slowly the knife is pressed into his flesh and he's killed in the most intimate and ghastly way. That officer's name was Corporal Upham.

For a few weeks after this, my nickname among the players was Private Upham. I laughed along, but inside I was burning in my stomach to change the perception.

6

Must Be the Irish in Me

Here's a revelation: the Murphys are Irish. Who'd have thought? I certainly never thought about it too much growing up. Occasionally I'd hear Mum or Dad play one of their Fureys CDs, and we watched *The Commitments* on VHS on repeat. Of course, I did realise we must be of Irish descent, Murphy being one of the most common names in Ireland, but the appetite to investigate any further didn't come to me until my mid-twenties.

As it happens, the Murphys come from the south: a place called Castleisland in County Kerry. You have to go back a few generations to find the Irish men and women on that side who boarded ships headed for Australia, but, like so many others, they did. And Mum is a Slattery and one of 14 children. It doesn't get much more Irish than that, does it? I have it on good authority that the Slatterys originate from the village of Tipperary in County Cork.

Born to Jack and Cassie Slattery, Mum was the fourth-youngest in a tribe of six boys and eight girls. She grew up on a farm in

Diggora, just outside Rochester in Victoria's northwest. There are a lot of stories from the sheep farm that Mum was raised on, but the one I love the most is of the little kids hopping in the back of a cart pulled along by a horse named Jinny. A canvas tarp was thrown over the kids to protect them from the elements, they'd give Jinny a little tap on the bum and she'd ferry them to school a few miles away. This was their school bus, if you could call it that. This went on for years, until one day Jinny fractured a bone in her hip as she passed through the school gate. Mum and her siblings were devastated as Jinny whined in pain all day outside the classroom window. The teacher kindly allowed the Slattery kids to leave class and comfort Jinny, on their own, throughout the day in shifts. Mum tells me that Jinny's mane soaked up the tears of a lot of little kids that day.

So there I was, Irish on both sides, bearing one of the most common surnames in Ireland, and with some gentle influences of Irish culture coming out of the family stereo and television on a daily basis. But somehow the penny hadn't dropped about my origins.

I remember the moment that all changed, in the backstreets of Dublin.

In 2002 I received a very late call-up for the Australian International Rules team. It was unexpected and a massive thrill. In a whirlwind week, I joined my teammates (many of whom were superstars of the game) for a quick training camp at Trinity College in Melbourne's east, then flew out of Melbourne. Life was moving fast and I loved every second of it.

After overcoming jetlag and acquiring a taste for Guinness, we got to work on the round ball. The training sessions on this trip were something to behold. It didn't matter what had happened the night before, how late you got home or how heavy your hangover was, the standard expected was incredibly high. All-star teams put together like this are a perfect mix of competitiveness and ego. No-one wants to be the dud.

Before we took on the Irish in front of 70,000 passionate locals in a two-test series at Croke Park, we had to overcome a local team that had been thrown together for our benefit. Dublin City welcomed us to their home ground on the edge of town. It looked like a pretty rough part of Dublin. As our bus rolled into the car park behind the pitch, a piercing *Whack! Whack! Whack!* sounded – something was ricocheting off the bus windows. I looked out to see five or six kids standing on a small embankment each with a rock in hand and arm cocked ready for launch. *Whack! Whack!* These cheeky little rascals were our unofficial welcome party.

I looked closer at the handful of ratbags and guessed that they ranged in age from six to about ten. With their mousey brown hair, red cheeks and freckle-dotted faces they looked ... familiar. Rewind a decade or so, and any one of them could have been me! *Oh boy, I really am Irish!*

I put this genealogical bombshell out of my head as we readied ourselves to play our first game with the hybrid rules and different-shaped ball. And there it stayed, until midway through

the game, when my Dublin City opponent took half a step back and read the name on the back of my guernsey.

'Murphy! You should be playing for us, ya COONT!'

It got better. A few minutes later it was my turn for a rest on the bench, and the punters decided to get involved. 'Murphy – you fookin' traitor! You're a fookin' tray-tor!'

In written form, this might read like a threat, but we all knew it was theatre: tongue-in-cheek sort of stuff. My big-name Australian teammates were all giggling. The evidence of my ancestry was mounting.

That two-week tour was one of the best experiences of my footy career. To be able to spend concentrated time with the game's elite in such a beautiful country was the thrill of a lifetime. I soaked up the culture of Dublin and Galway like a sponge and was regularly caught off-balance by the Irishness in me. It wasn't just the way I looked, it was everything – the humour, the music, the storytelling, the mood swings. It was all there!

For the first time, I realised how much Irish culture had seeped into our home through Mum and Dad. A lot of it came from the television we watched, but it was there. Walking the streets of Galway or sitting in a Dublin corner pub, I felt like a piece of a puzzle had just slotted into place. I was 21 years old, a young man finding my place in the AFL world, trying to balance those commitments with a growing thirst to be an individual and to find an outlet of creativity away from the game, still working out who I was. And suddenly I uncovered this whole other side of my soul that needed to be explored.

After we beat the Irish in front of their home crowd in the most amazing stadium I've ever played in, I came home and, yes, I think I had changed. The thrill of victory and of being the wide-eyed teammate of iconic AFL players was great, but the real change was more personal. Back in Melbourne, I found myself again and again turning to things that were undoubtedly Irish in spirit. I didn't get off the plane from Dublin and rush out to buy a stack of kitschy trinkets. But slowly, over the next 15 years, I became fascinated with Irish culture. I asked more questions of my parents about where our clan had come from. And I picked the brains of people like Martin Flanagan and Paddy Walsh, friends who had both spent good chunks of time in Ireland and had strong ancestral links to it themselves. I'd sit and listen to their stories like a small child.

And then of course there was the simple joy of sitting in a bar like The Drunken Poet in West Melbourne, listening to The Pogues on the jukebox, nursing a pint of Guinness, waiting for it to settle in its hypnotic way. In a sense I was a cliché, not unlike an Australian tourist riding a bicycle through Paris with a baguette in his basket. (For the record, I did that as well!) I feel right at home in the Poet. There are good Irish bars and there are crap imitations of what an Irish bar might look like. Then there's The Drunken Poet, an emerald gem of Melbourne. The Poet is run by a real Irish lass named Siobhan and I like to stop by every now and then. It's small, cosy and it's not a tourist bar. It's beautiful. On most days, there's music playing in the front corner, world-class Irish and folk music. It's a happy place for me.

Saturday, 2 May 2015: Sydney, preparing to take on the Swans

Last week we beat Adelaide at home by playing close to perfect football. We defended the whole ground with fanaticism and kicked a massive score. Some of our kicking through the middle of the ground was breathtaking. No doubt we caught the Crows off-guard; perhaps they underestimated us a touch. As impressive as it was, I'm sure a lot of punters and experts put it down to a flash in the pan – encouraging, yes, but not a seismic shift.

This week was always going to be a much more difficult assignment, and not just because we'd lost the element of surprise. Taking the Swans on at the SCG is always a formidable task, and in the wet and slippery conditions that are forecast, it's going to be that bit harder. The Swans traditionally love a scrap in the mud. I am also mindful that our young group might be a little bit too comfortable in the wake of last week's great win.

Thankfully, there haven't been any signs of complacency in the lead-up, and by the time we arrive in the Harbour City and drop in for a look at the ground, I am encouraged by the general buzz. I'm beginning to understand this group of players I'm leading each week: they play better if we keep things relaxed and loose. It's been an adjustment for me. For the past ten years, I've been coached by Rodney Eade and Brendan McCartney, both intense men, in different ways. A lot of us older blokes have been white-knuckling it for some time.

On the SCG for our Friday captain's run, the last training session before game day, the boys do their thing without incident. I keep one eye on Clay Smith, who is back in the senior team after his second knee reconstruction. I'm not alone: I think the group is concerned for Clay because he has no concern for himself when he plays. He's a tough customer. Hopefully he gets a good run at it.

We walk off the SCG just as drizzling rain begins to fall. As we take one more look out across the gorgeous cricket ground, one of the boys says, 'It's hard to believe that's the exact spot where Phil Hughes died.' It's a sobering moment – it's only been a few months since cricket's great tragedy.

All athletes are brave. To compete, you have to be willing to lose, and I don't think we give ourselves enough credit for that. But physical risk is also constant and I don't think many of us really think about it very often. Maybe we suppress it because, if we did think about it, it could ruin us as competitors. Just about every coach I've had over the years has used the phrase, 'You have to keep pushing yourself, put your bodies on the line, no-one is going to die out there.' Or words to that effect. Well, someone did die that day. Through a freak accident, a truly gifted young Australian batsman lost his life. I can't imagine the trauma for Phillip's teammates and opponents who witnessed the scene.

Our small group walks off in tender silence, sadness swishing around in our thoughts.

That night, after dinner and a massage in the hotel, we convene in one of the meeting rooms to go over tactics for tomorrow. Once the mechanics of the plan are explained and worked through, the talk turns to the other side of the game. The story. The emotion. The space between the spokes on the wheel. This is coach Luke Beveridge's meeting. One word is written on the whiteboard in bold capital letters: REVOLUTION.

Bevo asks someone from the group to offer a definition of the word and Tom Boyd answers without hesitation: 'A movement or shift in power from one group to another.' Bevo then talks about revolutions from history and the power of uprisings, emphasising that there is always a single moment or turning point when a revolution really takes hold. We can join the dots. Talk like this doesn't come without risk. Only two weeks ago, the night before we played the mighty Hawks in Tasmania, Bevo spoke at length about the David and Goliath fable. The next day we were breathing fire, only to lose two key players in the first quarter and go on to be crippled and slaughtered. Talkin' about a revolution is great, and I love every second of it. But what happens to this 'revolution' if we get rolled?

In the first ten minutes of the game, the Swans slash our tyres with two quick goals, but our boys keep pushing, running and linking up with chains of handball. All of a sudden, we kick a couple and we're going toe to toe. I feel the air return to our tyres. Wind can ruin a good game of footy, but slippery conditions can bring out the best in players. Physical courage is on full display and there are more opportunities to show it or avoid it; the players with the best ball skills rise to the top. We nudge our way in front, but only by a goal or two. Sydney, as expected, are up for the fight. They were never going to just hand it to us.

I've got my hands full down back with Craig Bird tagging me as a half-forward and the rest of the Swans making a point of elbowing me every time they run past. I take it as a compliment, and take a moment to play with the thought that I can have an impact for my team. When you're tagged as a half-back flanker, your natural reaction is often to run far and wide to get an easy kick to relieve the pressure, but I've been tagged enough from this part of the ground to know that there's a better way to get yourself into the game.

If Bird is going to follow me around, pushing into me every time the game stops, I'll take him to the contest. Take him to where I think the ball is going to end up. Because Bird is ultradefensive: he's not actively trying to find the ball on the lead. So, when the Swans have the ball, I try to read their kick, but I also play the percentages of who they like to kick the ball to: Buddy Franklin. Buddy is lurking in the forward 50, so I keep an eye on him, knowing that's where the ball will most likely end up. Get to the contest, win the ball or assist in winning it, and then run away from the congestion. This is very different to just running away for space all day, which is what Bird wants. I only know this because on the SCG three years ago, he shut me right out of the game. That was a wet day too. I won't let it happen again. Not this day.

At half-time we're two goals up and it's on. Neither side is taking a backwards step. As we emerge from the rooms and go through a quick warm-up, we come together as a group and I drag my teammates in close, hanging onto a couple of jumpers at random by the scruff of the neck.

'This could be one of the great wins in the history of our footy club, but we are going to have to hurt to get over the line. And I don't know about you, but I like the sound of a revolution!'

Like a lot of footy talk, my little sermon probably reads the same as every half-time huddle across the country. But that's why I like footy talk. It's its own genre in a way. There's a good chance close to half the group you're talking to aren't listening to what you're saying anyway. They'll remember the emotion and the spirit of the words, but ask them after the game for the specifics and you're likely to get an embarrassed or vacant look.

My sister got married quite young to a broad-chested Greek by the name of Ben Soumilas. She chose well. My brother in-law (known to all as Souma) played under a coach back at Garfield who swore *a lot*. Everything was 'Fuck this' and 'Fuck that', to the point that Souma had a chat with him about changing it up a bit. 'If you really want to emphasise something, use a word like 'imperative' or something like that,' Souma told him. The coach scratched his chin and seemed to like what he had heard. And sure enough, the next week, at quarter-time, the coach's sermon began with, 'It's fuckin' *imperative* we beat these cunts into the ground!'

Who knows what the lasting effect of those final few words before you break for play are, but as captain I take them very seriously and put as much into them as I can.

The second half is everything you would want to see in a game of footy. The best players from both sides are in the thick of it and influencing the game, but the role players and youngsters are also having an impact.

A game of footy is like a radio frequency that you have to tune into, and every week that frequency changes just a little. Sometimes the reception is gin clear, sometimes it's static. I don't know if I've ever had clearer reception than today. It's not that I'm best on ground, far from it, but I'm *inside* the game. I feel every bit of it and revel in its importance.

As the end draws nearer, I'm still the target for some off-the-ball niggle, but as the game tightens and the stakes go up and up, the petty bickering evaporates. This game is too good for that kind of posturing. Only Mike Pyke, the Canadian ruckman, keeps it up a little longer than anyone else. He tells me how he's going to rip me in half, but I just laugh and remind him that he's 'a friendly Canadian – your lot don't even lock your doors!'

At three-quarter time, the Bulldogs cling to a two-goal margin, but it's now officially a wet track and you can sense the Swans building a challenge. The last quarter will be a battle. Despite my Dogs never giving an inch or losing faith for a single moment, the Swans scratch out a couple of goals to nudge their way into the lead midway through the last quarter. It's not so much that they score, though – they trap the ball in their half for close to 20 minutes and our boys look tired. We're all exhausted. It pains me to say, but I've played in other teams where that effort and an honourable loss would have been enough.

But this is a different team coached by a new kind of coach. Our boys lift again. The last ten minutes of footy on that soggy SCG aren't pretty, but they are beautiful. The teams throw themselves into each other like a couple of drunken street fighters. The Swans had all the momentum, but suddenly it's ours again, and we keep pumping the ball into our forward line. Twenty-four minutes in, a Luke Dahlhaus snap out of a pack tumbles towards goal and looks like it might get there, before Easton Wood elects to jump high and kick the ball karate-style out of mid-air, as a Swans defender lunges. The obligatory score review is called for, while everyone holds their breath. Then: goal!

Two minutes to play and the Bulldogs hold onto a four-point lead. The desperation shown by both teams is the stuff of grand finals. Like a cross between an arm wrestle and mud wrestling, the game ebbs and flows from moment to moment – yes, no, yes, no. We somehow manage to trap the ball in our forward pocket with 17 seconds left. Surely that will be enough …

But the Swans still have one last card to play. Nick Smith takes the ball in the back pocket and with as much poise as you're ever likely to see on a football field, hooks it back into the corridor to find Jarrad McVeigh on his own. ON HIS OWN. Panic and adrenaline rip through our bodies, and the chase is on! With a few pairs of players and open space ahead of him, McVeigh kicks a tumble punt towards the Sydney forward 50. What happens in the next ten seconds will decide the result.

Easton Wood is first back, and despite the conditions and pressure, he picks the ball up cleanly. He's a star. Woody then shovels it to Jason Johannisen, who in turn flicks it over to Matty Boyd. Boydy is running on the spot, but he has just enough in his old legs to kick it off the ground and out of harm's way. Exhausted bodies in opposing jumpers are urging themselves after the ball as the siren goes.

WHAT. A. WIN.

Bulldogs players go in search of one another to hug, howl and roar. It's different to other wins, other close games – this is a win for the ages. Who knows what it will mean for the future? It feels like people in the stadium are shocked – not just by the result, but because of the drama and possibly because of the will of both teams. The Swans have been mighty and could have pinched it. But today is our day, and it's been a while since any of us at the Bulldogs could say that.

In the pandemonium of victory, Barry Hall, in his role as TV boundary rider, grabs me for a quick chat. He asks me to describe what it means. I fumble for the words. 'It's the best win, it's the greatest win I've ever been a part of. How can you not get emotional about footy?'

We stay out on the ground for longer than is customary, hugging and reliving the drama with each other, making our way over to the fence to touch hands and exchange exhilarated smiles with our travelling supporters. God knows they've been through a lot these past few years too. We walk off the soaked, emerald green

SCG and descend to our rooms, and our coach is waiting for us before we make it all the way in. With clenched fists, I scream 'COME ON!' Bevo throws his arms around me. It's instantly one of my all-time favourite footy memories.

You can tell a lot about a club and the importance of a win by the way they sing their theme song. For an experienced side who have picked up the chocolates as expected, you can get a sense of relief and of routine: 'We've won again, let's move on.' But today, for our team, it is anything but routine. We sing our tribal hymn like there is a chance we may never get to sing it again. We hold onto each other and the circle moves violently from side to side, back to front, like a moshpit. There is so much feeling in that circle. I've never heard our song sung like that before.

Something shifted today, I don't know what. Maybe this is what an injection of self-belief feels like. Perhaps it's more than that – maybe this really is the stuff of revolution.

7

Pre-Season Torture Camp

The 2003 season was a bad one for the Bulldogs. Wooden spoon bad. We won three games. Pre-season camps are always torturous, but the 2004 instalment that followed that grim year stands head and shoulders above the rest.

Later in my career, clubs would go off to all corners of the globe in search of altitude, heat and cultural sustenance. In the summer before the 2004 season, our coaches weren't seeking altitude per se, but there were mountains to be climbed. Apart from a list of generic clothing and equipment to bring, and the dates of the five days we'd be away from home, plans for the camp were cloaked in secrecy.

Curiously, on top of the list of things to bring was a fishing rod. Something smelt fishy all right.

Adam Cooney was our highly publicised recruit, taken with pick number one in the draft, and he'd been training with us for a week already. Farren Ray (who was taken with the fourth pick) had been given permission to head north with his mates for schoolies before joining the club. The Monday morning that we gathered at the Kennel to head off to camp was the first time any of us had laid eyes on Farren.

Just before six on Monday morning, the entire Bulldogs playing list filled the meeting room, and despite the sporadic laughter that usually bounces around a room full of footballers, there was unmistakable tension in the air. The sort of tension that got you thinking, 'I'm not sure we're going on a fishing trip.'

Sure enough, at precisely 6 am, three Special Operation Group (SOG) officers marched into the room in full black operations attire, guns on hips, and stared us down. There was ice in their eyes and, when they spoke, steel in their voices. Some guys laughed as a reflex; I wasn't one of them. I sensed this was going to be a week like no other. This was going to be brutal. The laughter died away as the SOG guys established very quickly who was in charge. These blokes are trained to kill the hardest criminals around. Intimidating a bunch of footballers was like shelling peas for them.

We were sent rushing out into the warm-up area, where we were marshalled into four teams. Coloured bibs numbered one through ten were handed out amid a palpable sense of panic. Red, white, yellow or blue. From now on, this was how each player was to be identified. I was no longer Robert Murphy, Bobby or Murph. I was Blue 5. Just as Peter Street was now White 5. Material things were worthless, reputations went in the bin. The only currencies of worth were discipline, push-ups and your appetite for pain.

Backpacks were quickly repacked to contain only the bare essentials. Not surprisingly, the fishing rods didn't make it. We were marched out on to Whitten Oval, where the SOG guys were waiting for us. As we clustered in our four groups, they screamed at us to do push-ups at whatever rhythm they saw fit. We were slaves, puppets to their every whim. I was already broken. I'd jumped into survival mode with both feet.

At some point during the first push-up torture session, we were instructed to quickly get up, grab our backpacks and get out to the car park, where our bus was waiting. We did as we were told, but it wasn't long until we found ourselves back in the push-up position – only this time with the loose asphalt cutting into our palms. I don't remember how long this went on, but by the end of it simply keeping your stomach off the ground felt like a hopeless goal. We were all twisting and contorting like fish in a bucket.

'Right! Get up! Stand up straight. On the bus!'

We dragged ourselves into the seats of the minibus that was idling nearby and took a moment to assess what had just happened. Heads were cocked and nervous smiles were exchanged among the playing group. Most of us were terrified. We were already knackered but we'd only been going for half an hour. How on earth could we survive five more days of this? Our hands were cut and our arms ached, but we knew things were surely going to get worse. The SOG guys were going to break us down. Already, you could have swept me up with a dustpan and brush. Blue 5 was in a world of hurt.

When we were physically able to speak again, the conversation turned to predictions of where we were going and what we were in for. Puckapunyal military base, in central Victoria, was a popular theory. But on this miserable Melbourne day, our bus wended its way through the streets of Port Melbourne and came to an abrupt stop next to the beach. We looked out at a grey and choppy sea.

Things were about to go up a gear.

The next two hours were utter hell. They remain the most physically challenging 120 minutes of my life. It started with us running the length of the pier and jumping into the ocean fully clothed, and things only got worse from there. Parts of that torture session remain a blur, but occasionally I have flashbacks of holding a heavy rope above my head in chest-deep swell, carrying logs, countless burpees in the sand, dips on the hand rails – and a few more push-ups, of course. Everything we did was strictly regimented, in our four coloured teams.

During one of the many push-up circuits, our SOG masters cranked up the verbal intimidation. I remember looking up for a moment to see one of them barking at Farren Ray, who was enjoying his first day in the AFL. 'Spent schoolies with your mates did ya, Farren? While all your teammates were down here training their guts out!' It was pretty brutal stuff and I felt bad for him, but I didn't think there was much I could do. I felt like a coward. I was a coward. And I had problems of my own: primarily, bringing shame to Blue team.

Shivering and exhausted, we were ordered onto our backs and on command had to do full sit-ups in unison. The only problem was that I couldn't do a full sit-up. For reasons that remain a mystery to me to this day, my abdomen had completely seized up. 'Blue 5! You call those sit-ups?!' The harder I tried, the less convincing it looked. I was stressing out. 'I can't fucking move,' was all I could say under my breath to defend my honour.

Lying next to me, laughing uncontrollably, was Simon Garlick (181-game player, future Western Bulldogs CEO, but on this day simply Blue 4). Garlo wasn't taking my abdomen seizure seriously at all. The Blue team eventually had to lock arms to finish the sit-ups because of my handicap. Blue 4 didn't stop laughing until we were done.

When I was drafted, I was eager to be accepted by the Bulldogs' senior players, and I clicked with Garlo from the outset. That said, one of our very first conversations was a bit frosty. I became aware that the other senior players would refer to Garlo as 'Ringy', so with us both lying head-down on the physio bed one day, I asked him why. He didn't lift his head, and gruffly replied, 'It's a long story.' As it turns out, it wasn't a long story at all. It was a short story. Garlo is a hairy man, like a ringtail possum. 'Ringy'. I must have got him on a bad day, because he's never been surly with me since.

I love Garlo. He was so good to me in those difficult early years and we're still very close. When we catch up, we don't so much chat as trade jokes and lines like stiff jabs to make each other laugh. There's a generosity to his friendship that is rare in this world and it's very precious to me. It crystallised for us that crazy day on Port Melbourne beach. During the torture session, the physical pain and exhaustion were so extreme they caused a growing level of hysteria. I mean, what we were doing was ridiculous. Young, athletic types who'd been rollerblading along Beach Road, weaving between pensioners walking their dogs, stopped and stared in stunned silence. We were being broken down physically and emotionally before their eyes. It was quite a scene.

Despite the trauma – and believe me, it was traumatic – the drill-sergeant language of the SOGs was just too much for Blue 4 and Blue 5. The more deliriously tired we became, the funnier the whole situation seemed. To ease the tension (at least in our own minds), Blue 4 and I started talking to each other in clichéd military lingo, a move which, if it had been overheard by one of the SOGs, would have been catastrophic. Finishing each sentence with a definitive 'SIR!' became our private joke.

One of the SOGs was an officer named Julian Seabrand, who was the biggest and also the youngest officer in charge of us. Blue 4 and I decided he was also the most handsome. Of all the military-flavoured demands and requests Blue 4 and I kept exchanging to amuse ourselves between sets of push-ups or commando crawls, the line I remember was 'Permission to find you attractive, SIR!' If a failure to count out the number of push-ups you were up to was a serious enough offence to warrant a punishment of 50 push-ups, how much was flirting with an officer worth? The trick, of course, was to have each other, but not the SOGs, hear the flirtatious remarks. It was risky, childish and exhilarating. We laughed our way through much of the physical pain. The cocktail of fatigue and hysteria was a close relative of insanity. We were teetering on the edge.

Years later, when Garlo became CEO of the Bulldogs, I was incredibly proud of him. At times, people in the footy club would watch us when we were around each other during work hours, because they knew how close we were. We played the parts of CEO and player seriously, but occasionally, if we bumped into each other in the corridors with no-one watching, we'd dissolve into laughter or wrestle each other and slip back into mock military speak. 'Permission to find you attractive, SIR!' When Garlo resigned as CEO at the end of 2014, I was saddened, and I missed him as the club rose from the ashes to win the 2016 premiership. He'd had a big hand in setting it all up.

The madness of that Port Melbourne beach chapter of the camp lasted for over two hours: could have been four, felt like about 12. But eventually it was over. We were wet, ragged and utterly spent. Officer Seabrand never caught wind of our growing affection for him, which was a little win for the Blue team. We shuffled back onto the bus and slumped back in our chairs with a thud. I couldn't stop thinking, 'What the fuck has all this got to do with playing football?'

In relative silence, the bus pulled away from the beach and headed west. The open road rocked a few boys to sleep, but I was too wired. When it came to ball sports, I was always a kid who could just play. I had confidence. But this camp was a whole different ball game. I was out of my depth and I had a genuine fear that I wouldn't be able to endure the week. I wasn't the only one reeling, but at that point I didn't really care about anyone else. I had to dig deeper, down into my soul, to find some resolve there that I wasn't sure existed. I was surrounded by teammates but I felt alone. It was a terrible feeling. There's nothing quite as scary as loneliness when you're in a crowd.

Eventually, the bus left the freeway and headed into a forested abyss. Gulp. We snaked our way up the country roads into the hills and heavy bushland. We passed a road sign that landed with a thud in our stomach. 'Mount Disappointment, 2 kilometres.' The irony wasn't lost on any of us.

The torture went on for two and a half days, but over that time I felt my resilience get stronger and stronger. I leaned on my teammates and they leaned on me too. After they broke us down, the SOGs spent the rest of the week conducting various team-building activities with us, including abseiling down cliff faces of a few hundred feet. That camp left a few scars, but in a good way. Callouses on the soul to use as armour. I couldn't have got through it if it wasn't for Blue 4, and that is what pre-season camps are all about. Flirting with military officers.

8

Playing Tall

For a few years in the middle of the 2000s, I played as an undersized, unconventional centre half-forward for the Bulldogs. It was unexpected, but I'd had a taste of it before. For one football season back in 1998, I had played centre half-forward in the Warragul Under 16s under coach Mick Gargan. To say I was undersized is an understatement – I was a skinny wingman! But Mick saw something in me as a player that no-one else had up until that point. That year was one of the most enjoyable I had playing footy, and it was a great bonding experience for me and my brother too.

It was Mick's plan to play me as centre half-forward and he was full of good methods, but it was my brother, Ben, who taught me how to play the position. He would watch me play and we'd talk about 'space'. Where was there space on a footy ground? How do you create space? My brother knows his footy and has gone on to coach at suburban level. He coached East Brighton to a premiership a few years ago and now holds the reins at Seaford Football Club.

At my size, I had to be able to move, so space became very important. Simple things like standing at least 20 metres away from a stoppage and 20 metres inside the boundary line for a throw in were just a couple of ways I could create space. More often than not, the ball would tumble out of the pack along the skinny or boundary side of the ground. The more space I'd created before that moment, the more room I had to use my speed to gather the ball and get away from my opponent. Anything to avoid getting caught in a wrestle with a bigger, stronger opponent.

It's funny in this game how things come back around ...

When Rodney 'Rocket' Eade took over as the senior coach at the Western Bulldogs, he hatched a plan to move me forward again. Rocket took over in 2004, after a disastrous few seasons. He was renowned as a sharp tactician with a harsh tongue and quit wit. I loved playing under Rocket, especially in the early years of his time at the Bulldogs. He could be very hard on players, but he was a charismatic storyteller too and we started winning games. That always helps. Rocket was an unconventional coach in some ways. He plotted my move from the back flank to centre half-forward in early 2005, after our captain, Luke Darcy, went down with a serious knee injury. Darce made his name as a ruckman, but he was also a clever and damaging forward. Just prior to his knee injury, Darce had terrorised opposition teams with his strong leading and accurate goal-kicking. When he went down, he left a big hole. Always thinking outside the box, Rocket hatched a plan to fill our forward line with a group of small- and medium-sized players – myself included. It was a plan that was pretty light on 'structure and process' and pretty big on 'talent and work rate'. We often used the phrase 'organised chaos' to capture what it was we were trying to achieve. In our day, we could trouble any side in the competition, and we kicked some big scores. For a team that had been down the bottom of the ladder for the last few years, it was exhilarating to be winning games regularly and playing a style of footy and in a line-up that was different to every other team in the competition. I felt like I'd finally found my niche in the league as a hard-running, mark-on-the-lead player. Much of what I had learnt from my Under 16s year held strong.

Playing centre half-forward at 187 cm (6'1") and 80 kg had some unexpected benefits. These were still the days when your opponent at the start of the game generally remained your opponent for most of the day, and he followed you. In future years, the best defenders and best defensive units would stand out in front of you, which changed the aesthetic of the game. A lot more goals are now kicked 'out the back', over the top of these aggressive defensive formations.

In 2005 the defenders went where you went, generally playing you from your back shoulder, giving you freedom to lead at the ball. This suited me just fine.

Often I found myself with a centre half-back as an opponent who was used to playing on the power forwards like Warren Tredrea or Matthew Pavlich. One of the football lessons I kept tucked into my top pocket was from my formative years as a half-back flanker.

Playing against Sydney one day, it was my job to mind Ryan O'Keefe and I was staggered to see just how far he was willing to run to take marks on the lead. He ran me ragged, and as unpleasant as it was, I couldn't help but admire his heart.

When I got my turn to play forward, it was the O'Keefe model I based my game on. This fit perfectly with what the team needed, but there was also a dignity in playing this way that appealed to me. I thought of it as an honourable way of playing the game. I wanted to run long and hard and take as many marks as I could and then bring my teammates into the game. It was a simple philosophy, but it's a simple game. Sometimes.

Instead of moving the ball slowly and predictably in straight lines to our key position players, Rocket's Bulldogs moved the ball on diagonal lines with risky, exciting kicking to leading players. We had players who could run fast and kick sweetly, and this style suited me down to the ground. I began to relish the start of the games, when these big, tough centre half-backs (think Dean Solomon, Chad Cornes and co.) would make their way over and stand next to me. It wouldn't take long before they'd start to try to push me around. Then as soon as the game started, I'd try to run them and myself into the ground.

'Organised chaos' meant nothing if you didn't push yourself to exhaustion. I found an appetite for covering the ground that I never had as a floating half-back flanker. Taking chest marks up on the wing became like a drug: I was hooked. In 2005, I kicked 33 goals and took 172 marks (the fifth most in the competition; Matthew

Richardson was sixth with 166). In 2008 I took 208 marks (fourth most) and kicked 34 goals.

They weren't all good days though. In the dying moments of a game against the Crows at Football Park in round five, 2006, I'd gone up for a mark in the middle of the ground and when I came down I rolled my ankle. It was your bog standard, garden-variety rolled ankle that every player has endured. Moments later the siren sounded and I gingerly limped from the field knowing I'd be touch and go to get up for the next week against the Saints. As you do, I assumed no-one had noticed my little ankle tweak.

Rolled ankles are pretty sore for a couple of weeks, but with a bit of tape and some gritting of teeth you can get through. When the Bulldogs ran out at Docklands the following weekend against the Saints, I was sore but strapped up and ready to play. At the opening bounce, I stood at centre half-forward waiting to see who would stand by me for the day, when veteran St Kilda defender Max Hudghton bounded over to me like a hyperactive Doberman. He was all verbose body language and elbows in my ribs. And then it started ... He began tapping my ankle with the toe of his boot. He wasn't kicking me, it was just an unfriendly tapping: clearly he knew about my ankle. He was trying to intimidate me. He did intimidate me. I felt a wave of dread crash over me.

Sore ankles aside, I've never been given a bath like the one Max Hudghton gave me that day. I wilted in the face of his superior athleticism and will. He wore me so closely that at times it felt like we were playing in the same pair of shorts. At this time I usually got a mismatch of some kind, but on that day I ran into an opponent who was bigger, stronger, faster, more disciplined *and* nastier.

I learnt a few good lessons that day, and vowed never to wilt like that again.

Saturday, 12 September 2015: Adelaide

Losing elimination finals always feels like a kick in balls, but I'm absolutely gutted after tonight's loss to the Crows. Our season had felt like a magic carpet ride. I truly believed we could go all the way this year, and I know Bevo believed we could too. Maybe we didn't have enough players who also believed.

The game was a belter, or so I've been told. It was an entertaining, high-scoring game. End-to-end football. But I don't give a shit about any of that. I can barely remember the details, because it all moved so quickly. I'm sure it was great to watch, but the game wasn't played in a style that went to plan for my Bulldogs. We've let a golden opportunity pass us by.

It was weird out there tonight. All year, our tactics at the centre bounces have confused opposing teams. We know the plans that Bevo gives us inside out, and I've become accustomed to watching other teams scramble at centre bounce because of our refusal to follow their numbers. Bevo has an unwavering belief in himself and us as a team. At times, he doesn't mind if we play with only five defenders against six forwards. That is radical! It's part of the reason we love him so much. He's a football optimist. But tonight, the Crows were always one step ahead with the human battleships of the strategy. It was as if they knew what we were about to do. They were calm at the restart of play, every time. That hasn't happened all year.

I'm tired. Exhausted. I just can't stop going over in my mind the chance we've let go to waste. Sitting here trying to make sense of it all, I can hardly believe our season is over. I feel like a soldier who's had his arm blown off but still has the sensation of that arm, his hand and his fingers. My body and brain are trained to reload. There's always next week, only this week there isn't.

It's only when your campaign is done that you look back on the year and realise just how much hard work goes into getting to that position. Now is not the time to think too far ahead – I don't have the energy – but you start to wonder whether you've got it in you to go through it all again. The fatigue takes control of your thoughts ... No, this team is on the rise and we'll go again next year. But right now I've got a taste in my mouth like battery acid.

Postscript: In the weeks following Adelaide's elimination final win over the Bulldogs, the AFL investigated whether Bulldog Michael Talia, who had been dropped for the elimination final, had passed information about the Dogs' game plan to his brother, Adelaide Crow Daniel Talia. Michael Talia was traded to Sydney midway through the two-month investigation and the Talias were cleared of any wrongdoing.

9

Finding My Voice

In some ways, I look back on the early years of my footy career and I'm pleasantly surprised that I didn't rebel in the typical sense. I only drank alcohol after games: I never went out during the week. Apart from the time in 2001 when I swore at Nobes, I never willingly disobeyed my coaches, but I did felt restrained at times by the conservative and strict nature of the footy club.

I'm not an extrovert by nature, but occasionally I do very extroverted things. I think I get that risk-taking urge from my mum. I once dressed up as a choirboy and sang a hymn on a TV show. It's on the internet, you can check it out (you'll notice it's in the wrong key). And in 2003 I scrawled 'NO WAR' on my forearm before we posed for the annual team photo in the pre-season. The week before, there had been a march in the city protesting against Australia's participation in the war in Iraq. I'd wanted to go along, but my schedule wouldn't allow it, so I did that instead. Simple.

But I did know it would stir the pot, and I was right. My little foray into the world of international politics got some media attention and was condemned by the AFL: they brought in a rule forbidding players from making political statements. The club captain at the time was Chris Grant, who defended me. I'm paraphrasing, but Chris said to the media, 'I thought the reason we were fighting this war was to protect freedom of speech.' What a man.

Both within my own club and in the football world at large, I was stamped as being 'a bit out there'. But I didn't really mind; to a degree, that's why I did it. I didn't want to be just a footballer.

The full force of my actions was felt later, though. I was often pressed and pushed in interviews for my views on politics. I'm not a political animal. I wasn't then and I'm not now. Occasionally an issue sparks my passion and I'll let it rip, but I always read the paper from the back – even once I started writing for it.

I was a restless soul before I started writing for *The Age* in 2007. I've always loved the game, but conforming to its rigid structure tested me a lot. I didn't realise how much I craved a creative outlet until I started penning a weekly column on footy and life in Melbourne. Our football manager at the time was Matthew Drain, and one day he asked me, 'Would you consider writing for *The Age*?' I shake my head in amazement at the memory now, but with almost no thought at all I just said, 'Yep.' I barely considered what it entailed, nor did it immediately dawn on me what a lucky break it was. Journalism students must hate my guts. I did hear from my management company around this time that ten players had turned down the offer of writing for the broadsheet newspaper, but that was surely just a rumour.

There were quite a lot of missteps in those columns, especially in the early years, but I soon fell in love with the craft. I copped some criticism, of course, like the woman who sidled up behind me in a Borders bookstore and whispered in my ear, 'You're not as interesting as you think you are.' But others people were more encouraging.

I believe in fate, and as a budding young columnist I was handed over to Peter Hanlon, who would mentor me and help me with the column. It wasn't a ghostwriting partnership of the sort favoured by most, if not all, players. I treated my writing like an apprenticeship. Peter, or Tommy as he is affectionately known, was and still is a great mentor to me. Everything I've ever written has been shown to him first. You need a lot of trust in that kind of relationsip. He's a good man to ride the river with.

In my early days at *The Age*, Tommy sent me a collection of columns written by former Blues, Roos and Demons superstar Brent Crosswell. There were about a dozen columns and every one of them was a classic. In that regard, the Crosswell columns are a bit like the 12 episodes of *Fawlty Towers*. That was the standard I was chasing.

Every so often someone would describe my writing as 'Irish'. This pleased me greatly for a couple of reasons, the main one being that it happened by accident. I haven't read much Irish writing, so I wasn't able to copy an Irish style even if I wanted to. Truthfully, I didn't really know what I was doing. I was writing purely on instinct. It was from the gut. I was just following my nose. But enough people whose opinions mattered to me supported the theory that my instincts as a writer were indeed very Irish. Australia's most famous bard, Paul Kelly, was kind enough to endorse a collection of my newspaper columns that ended up in a book titled *Murphy's Lore*. Paul's endorsement finished with the line, 'it could be the Irish in him'. I put it on the cover.

*

I've always agreed with this piece of wisdom from Nick Hornby's novel *High Fidelity*: 'What matters is *what* you like, not what you *are* like.' It's an especially good philosophy when it comes to filling out a player profile.

The *Footy Record* player profile is a bit of a lost art form for the modern footballer, much to my disappointment. With a little bit of thought it can be an entertaining ride. Sadly, most players fall into the clichéd rhythm of those who have gone before them. If we were to track the garden-variety footballer of the last 30 years, we'd get a very mainstream (yet satisfactory), slightly bland lineage of the player profile 'Big 6': *Lethal Weapon, Braveheart, The Shawshank Redemption*; Cold Chisel, Powderfinger, Coldplay.

Don't get me wrong, I love me a bit of Chisel. And who could forget Andy Dufresne crawling through 500 yards of excrement for his freedom? But players who tread this well-worn path tell me very little about themselves, except maybe that they haven't put aside enough time to adequately cater to the needs of the curious footy fan with a bent for indie snobbery.

Players have missed games for the birth of a child; I'd be prepared to miss a game if I had a player profile in front of me with a deadline. I always likened the player profile to a message in a bottle thrown out to sea. You put pen to paper to record the movies, songs and people that fill your dreams, and send it out into the world with the vague hope that maybe one day it'll wash up on a shore somewhere and into the loving arms of a special someone.

On the eve of the 2008 AFL season, I sat down at my locker at the footy club to scrawl my annual *Footy Record* opus, bottle and cork at the ready. When I got to the centrepiece of all player profiles – the dream dinner guests – I strategically named three: Tim Rogers, Tex Perkins and Gus Agars.

I cheated a little bit, because Gus was my newest friend at the time. Gus is a rock'n'roll drummer of some repute, who dropped into my local pub from time to time, and we had a few mutual friends. It wasn't exactly Keith and Mick at the train station with a couple of blues records, but it was a bit like that. We hit it off immediately.

Gus has played the backbeat for Tim, Tex, Paul Kelly, the Gin Club, Marlon Williams and just about every other Melbourne band that I've loved. I have a theory about Melbourne's rock'n'roll scene. As far as I can tell there's about 12 or 13 musicians, and from that baker's dozen there are about 65 bands. Shape shifters. Anyway, Gus was my mate, and him being a mad Kangaroos fan I thought he might get a kick out of seeing his name in the *Footy Record*, so in he went. Tim and Tex went in for similar reasons, but I'd be lying if I didn't admit there was a tiny part of me that thought, 'It's not beyond the realms of possibility for these dinner party guests to one day break bread together.'

In the middle of that season Gus invited me to Tiamo on Lygon Street. Waiting at the table were T'n'T – Tim Freakin' Rogers and Tex Goddamn Perkins. My plan had worked, my message in a bottle had been carried to friendly shores, the player profile was alive!

I wondered if this had ever happened before? Had an AFL player ever walked into Tiamo to find Nelson Mandela, Robbie Williams and Pamela Anderson thumbing through the menu? I reckon we'd have heard about it. So I might be the first and only player to have dinner with his dream dinner guests.

I felt a little bit embarrassed as we settled in as a cosy foursome, but it didn't take long to find our rhythm. My dream dinner guests all like to eat and talk, so things moved at a rapid pace. We swapped stories from the road and the field. I got the giggles when Tim ordered chicken livers for his main course. I'm still intrigued by that. It was such a treat to sit with my rock'n'roll heroes, and I think they got a kick out of making my dream a reality.

I told them of a run-in I'd had with Gary Ablett Jr a few weeks earlier, in which little Gary spat at me: 'You're just a mouth, Murphy.' I took away a few things from Tiamo that night – a bucketlist dinner party, a new nickname (The Mouth), and a crash course in a game called Zoneball.

Tucked away in the corner of the crowded restaurant, Tex talked animatedly about the genesis of this sport he'd personally created, its rules, its traditions. At the end of our dinner it was hugs and smiles all round. Plans were made to meet for a game of Zoneball over summer. And meet up we did, and it was brilliant. There have been other dinners too; at a steakhouse in St Kilda one night, Tim ordered seven oysters. Not half a dozen or a dozen. Seven. I'm not sure if he orders these things just to mess with me, or if he is a psychedelic culinary wizard.

A fondness endures among this quartet. It's not so much a list of dream dinner guests these days as a simple booking for four, which is nice. There are always plans for another dinner down the track and big plans for Zoneball. I once asked Tex if he could capture the essence of his gift to sport, and this is what he had to say: 'Zoneball is a game invented by bored musicians, and is basically a cross between footy and tennis. It was codified by Tex Perkins on 14 October 2001. Popular with cripples, musos and comedians, it can be played while drunk (the one-handed aspect of the game allows players to drink, smoke or eat as they play). It is truly the game of the 21st century.'

Amen to that.

Someone once said to me that most rock'n'rollers want to be footballers and most footballers want to be rock'n'rollers. There's plenty of evidence to support the theory, and I've certainly tried as hard as anyone to infiltrate both worlds. A few years back I was asked if I would be assistant coach for the Espy Rockdogs in the Community Cup that plays annually against the PBS Megahertz. I said 'yes' in a flash. I was the right-hand man for the senior coach, Paul Kelly. I was very happy to be the second banana.

Before the game, we met at Paul's place in St Kilda for a cup of tea before making the walk to Elsternwick Park. As we marched the footpaths and backstreets of Elwood, Paul asked me if he could run through his pre-match address. Paul spoke with poise as he recited his prepared monologue without referring to any notes, at one point paying homage to Elvis Presley and the fire lit by The King for all rock'n'rollers to follow. I've had my fair share of highlights and poignant moments in life, but that walk is right up there near the top.

The Community Cup is a curious beast. I've been as a punter in the outer and I've been in the inner sanctum and I'm still a little unsure if it's taken seriously or if it's a piss-take. The ambiguity is a strength of the event. As we hit our stride on the pavement, though, I'll never forget the moment Paul thanked the opposition. Without them, he said, 'we don't have the gift of competition'. I'd never heard someone put it like that before.

What a treat it was to have a private performance from the great bard himself, albeit a spoken word one. It made me smile all the way to the game. Paul and I catch up sporadically for cups of coffee or a kick of the footy. I admire his drop kick and his discipline to leave every half volley, something of a signature for all touring musicians. Jarred or broken fingers are kryptonite to their magic as song-and-dance men and women.

When Justine turned 29 a few years back I thought it would be fun to record Paul's song, 'You're 39, You're Beautiful and You're Mine' on a cassette for her as a gift, changing the lyric to '29' (genius, I know).

I rang Gus and asked how we could go about it. 'Nothing fancy,' I said, just a tape-deck demo that hopefully charms my girl with its amateurish but genuine heart. Gus, who is enthusiastic by nature, jumped into the project with both feet.

I was called to an address in Northcote, the home of multi-instrumentalist and all-round good guy Dan Luscombe, and I walked in to find the boys had set up the recording equipment. It was then that I found out that Dan had played the piano on the original recording! It was all starting to look and sound a bit too professional until it was time for the singer to add his vocals. The singing was pretty diabolical, but I gave it everything I had and it was one of the most enjoyable nights of my life.

Things got a bit boozy, and when Gus added a hidden line at the end of the chorus, a creepy, whispering 'I love you Justine', we were all giggling like schoolgirls. Almost a year later I got a text from Paul Kelly. 'Hey, I heard your singing, sounded good.'

Sunday, 14 January 2016: Northcote

Scotty West used to say, 'It's easier to stay fit than it is to get fit.' It took me a long time to see just how right he was.

Getting yourself physically ready to compete at AFL level can take years. Partly because, in a physical sense at least, footballers are jacks of all trades but masters of none. We need to be fast and able to cover long distances, as well as build our bodies up to endure the hits of combat when the ball is in dispute. All of these requirements must be teamed with the skills of the game. Feet, hands, hand–eye, hand–foot, danger all around you. But as pure athletes, we fall just short in lots of areas compared with Olympians, triathletes and the like. We are a constant disappointment to yoga instructors for our lack of flexibility, but no-one else can do what we do.

Who's to say what the most demanding sport in the world is? It's enough to know that this game demands everything you've got.

When players reminisce about pre-season training, the conversation is usually accompanied by an uncomfortable shiver. Long, hot summer days being pushed to the limits of your endurance and pain threshold leave a few scars, but I must admit I've grown to love it. That wasn't the case early on. It's a familiar tale, I suppose, but when you're not yet strong enough to endure the training load, every effort feels painful. Nauseating.

One thing I found is that all you need is someone doing it tougher than you to give your step a little pep. Each year a bunch of new pups join the club, and after a few days they wilt in the sun like dried-out roses. It feels almost sadistic to admit, but that sight can be enough to give a veteran a little shot in the arm.

This is my 17th pre-season. It's a jarring number if I sit and think about it. The daily droplets of my sweat have formed a reservoir. Having endured all of that work, having hardened the mind through years of punishment, I now get a rather perverse enjoyment out of the fatigue. When you're starting out or you're at the beginning of a new campaign and not quite as fit as you'd like to be, the training can feel like poison filling your legs and lungs. But with time, the hurt morphs into something else. It's not that the pain leaves you, just that it's balanced out by something pleasurable.

I suppose there's a scientific reason for this; the release of endorphins into the body is the 'natural high' sports scientists (or 'phys-edders', as former AFL CEO, Andrew Demetriou, once called them) speak about. The moments of physical euphoria are only fleeting, but that makes them even more precious. Thinking now about the feeling of pouring water on the back of my head at the end of today's session, I get butterflies in my stomach. John Mellencamp knows what I'm talking about – it hurt so good.

I read in Bruce Springsteen's autobiography, *Born to Run*, that he trained hard as a way of keeping his clinical depression at bay. His outlet was lifting heavy weights. In his own words, this left him 'too tired to be depressed'. I found that really interesting. I don't suffer from debilitating mental illness, but I can appreciate how the fatigue of exercise can simplify your life.

I'm sitting here right now with my aching legs stretched out on the couch. Having just eaten two meals, I'm too tired to sleep, too exhausted to move. It's a beautiful feeling. Pre-season, in particular, simplifies your life. You train, eat and recover. Train, eat and recover. Logic tells you that the repetition would become boring, but I've found it to be the complete opposite. It's like physical poetry. There are some days and moments that don't inspire me, of course, but for the most part, it relaxes me. I'm 34 years old, coming off my best year as a player, and I feel stronger than I ever have. In my private moments, I can't help but wonder if I'll be able to play forever. I feel faster now than I did when I was 21. I don't know if that's normal.

I read Ben Cousins' explosive autobiography a few years back, and at one point he described the feeling of peak fitness as 'feeling dangerous'. This morning, before the physical torture, I felt dangerous. When I'm somewhere near my physical peak, just walking isn't enough. I want to be let off the leash to run, like a greyhound.

I don't meditate; I have done in the past, but I didn't keep it up. Preparing for training and games of football function as my meditation. Packing my bag the night before, planning food and taking my vitamins: all these are rituals to serve the body. Getting to training early to stretch is the same. It's quiet, repetitive and peaceful.

I'm grateful I got to play long enough to fully appreciate the joy of being completely swallowed up by the demands of the game. The physical and the spiritual in partnership amid the chaos of the game.

10

My Knee Goes 'Pop'

The MCG turf beneath me was moist, and I lay in a prone daze. I hadn't seen it coming. Moments earlier, in the blur of play, the ball had been shunted along the ground in my direction. As I took possession, I was wrapped up in a heavy tackle from Collingwood powerhouse Anthony Rocca.

'Keep your feet' had served me fairly well as a mantra up to this point, but as I stubbornly tried to dig my feet into the ground and keep my legs rigid, the laws of physics conspired against my knee joint. Rocca picked me up, twisted my body and slammed me into the ground. My feet stayed where they'd been, and my left knee was ripped apart.

When the medial and anterior ligaments ruptured, the sound I heard in my head was like the violent tear of Velcro. The sideways jolt reminded me of ripping the leg away from the body of a roast chook. Pain poured into the back of my knee – not as sharp as a broken bone, more like a throbbing ache. Then nothing. No pain. No sound.

I knew enough about wrecked knees to understand that if the pain disappears you're in big trouble. I was still lying on my back on the MCG when the Bulldogs' doctor, Gary Zimmerman, performed 'the test'. 'The test' is what footballers call the Lachman – a two-handed physical jolt of the knee joint (preferably performed by a doctor or surgeon) to see whether the anterior cruciate ligament (ACL) is intact. To prove that, the jolting motion must have an endpoint. Zimmerman's words merely confirmed what I already knew. Trainers, medicos and physios looked down at me with an ocean of worry in their eyes. I looked past them, and all I could see was a clear, black sky.

I was in shock, no doubt, but a different panic was growing inside me. I struggled to recall the moments before the tackle, and was filled with dread that I'd flinched at the critical moment. My knee was wrecked; I'd miss a year of football. In 2006 the Bulldogs were on the rise and I felt I was going places too – now that was in jeopardy. But in that lonely moment, surrounded by 68,000 people, one question stung even more than that: did I just dog it? Hawthorn's Brad Sewell once wrote that a footballer's greatest fear is to show fear itself. If I'd just pulled out – dogged it – what would people be saying about me? What would people write? Would my teammates be ashamed of me?

As the stretcher slowly rolled across the field of play, I kept my gaze on the blankness of the sky, trying to keep the heaving panic at bay. Right on cue, a young Magpie supporter who looked about nine years old leaned over the fence and yelled in my face:

'Murphy – you fucked my dream team!' Even given his youth, it felt a touch harsh.

Down in the rooms, our club surgeon, David Young, walked me through the first phase of my rehabilitation, but I was only barely present. I was uncomfortably numb. I only really began to feel upset when a small group of players and coaches came into the room. Luke Darcy leaned against the wall. He looked devastated. Luke and I had always been very close, ever since he'd driven me to training in those first weeks at the club. I looked up to him. Now I saw fear and doubt in Luke's eyes: that would torment me for the next few years. In that moment, the shock subsided and a darker reality began to settle.

I sat in the dugout for the second half, but I don't remember much about the rest of the game. Collingwood ended up winning despite a gallant effort from the Dogs. My teammate and best friend, Daniel Giansiracusa, drove me home. It was a short and quiet trip. As we snaked past Fitzroy Gardens, I broke the silence by asking the question that had rattled around my head for the last two hours, haunting me.

'Just before I hurt my knee, did I pull out?'

To my eternal relief, Danny scoffed and said, 'No, mate, you were just unlucky.'

I'd never felt such relief in my life.

With the help of crutches, I limped inside to find my girlfriend in tears and in a state of shock too. Only a few months before, Justine and I had finally become a couple. We had always stayed in touch over the years. Both of us had been in relationships with other people, but we still kept an eye on one another, I suspect. When Justine moved back to Victoria, having lived in Queensland for a few years, we made time for one another. It started innocently with cups of tea, then led to pots of beer in the Lord Newry pub in North Fitzroy. After a few months, we took the next step and soon after, Justine moved into my two-bedroom cottage.

Everything had been going so well. And now this.

*

After Anthony Rocca's brutish tackle, with the insides of my knee ripped apart, I had surgery. Due to the damage to the knee I had to wear a heavy brace for a few months. For two weeks I was stuck on the couch at home watching movies and urinating in a plastic bottle. To fight off the boredom and the blues, Justine and I took a month-long trip through Europe during the middle of the season. We flew to London, where my brother was living, and then met friends in Edinburgh. From there, we travelled by train down to Paris and, with Bordeaux hangovers, snaked our way through the Riviera and on to Italy. With bellies full of pizza, pasta and rosé, we flew to Vienna for a few nights exploring a truly romantic city. Our final destination was Santorini in the Greek islands.

It was a magical trip – free from the shackles of football and its professional demands, free from the depressing forecast of my wrecked knee, and right in that sweet spot of a relationship where you are too busy laughing at each other's jokes to have children. It was a romantic time in our lives.

Santorini was stunning. And that came as a revelation, because when the plane touched down it seemed pretty underwhelming. Most of the island is desolate rubble, and the commute from the airport to the cliff-side is a 30-minute trip through weeds and discarded cinder blocks. But slowly the cab ascended higher and higher behind the cliff-top and the iconic white stone villages started to peek through. With tension building, thinking that this holiday destination might be a total bust, we got our suitcases out of the cab, walked through a concrete archway and were slapped in the face by the beauty of a shimmering Aegean blue. If there's a prettier view in the world I haven't seen it. Walking through a pristine white concrete maze to our villa, all we could do was smile and gawp. This would be our home for the next seven nights.

We lived a Greek paradise every single day. Sleep-ins, long lunches, frappés, cocktails, gyros, swimming, reading, sunbaking, saganaki and about a thousand Greek salads. It was pure heaven. The only reminder of any stress in our lives was my knee brace and limp.

Then I ruined it. One night, we returned to our villa after a long day of swimming, eating and drinking in the neighbouring village. It was only a short 15-minute walk with a limp, but when we got home we were a little bit drunk. It was also hot (apparently quite common in the Mediterranean). As Justine tottered off to bed I went downstairs to our little private pool to cool off. I stood on the edge of the pool and looked out across the darkened horizon. It was beautiful in any light, especially moonlight.

With as much thought as a hiccup, I dropped into the pool. I was nine weeks post-surgery. I landed with a perfect pin-drop, shot straight down through the water like a spear dropped from above, and both of my feet hit the bottom of the pool in synchronicity. The pool wasn't quite as deep as I remembered, but there was no twist, no hyperextension. The only thing that happened was both of my legs absorbed the impact, and because I had a sore knee from the operation I got a bit of biting pain as the left knee flexed further than it wanted to.

Even more bizarrely, when I got out of the pool, I knew all of that. I shook off the discomfort and gave my knee a bit of a rub, not thinking much of it. Then I headed up the stairs and into bed.

As I drifted in and out of sleep the following morning, I became dully aware of my hangover and had a flickering sense of regret and dread. That dread continued to build, and with each little snooze I'd wake up to find it more consuming than before. I started to replay the previous night's swim in my head, over and over and over again. I look back on this day as a brief trip into temporary insanity.

Eventually I woke up Justine, in a complete state of panic. Gone were the memories of a quick dip in the pool and the attendant moment of soreness. In its place were a whole new batch of memories and consequences. I was sure I'd wrenched my knee; the ACL was gone. Again. I'd be on the front page back home as the biggest fool in AFL history: 'Drunk Dog Wrecks Knee Again in Island

Paradise'. Gulp. Young people do dumb things and then they panic: this pindrop was my masterful contribution to the trend. Justine tried to calm me down and get me to explain what had happened, but by this point I was a raving lunatic.

So I asked her to do 'the test'.

Justine is an intelligent woman, a naturopath by trade who has a wide-ranging skillset and has worked in a number of fields. She's wonderful, the love of my life. But she is not a doctor. That didn't stop me asking her to do a quick Lachman test on our bed in our Santorini villa. What a scene. I think I even groaned in frustration when she complained that she couldn't do it. How ridiculous. Of course she couldn't execute a Lachman – it's a technical medical procedure.

Always the voice of reason in our relationship, Justine suggested we go for a walk to get coffee and see how the knee felt after a gentle stroll. As we walked through the white walls, my knee was a bit sore, but it felt stable. Still, that didn't stop me looking out across the horizon of the Aegean and wondering aloud, 'Maybe I should just jump off this cliff…'

It was at this point that Justine took control of the situation. I paraphrase, but she told me bluntly: 'Shut the fuck up and get your shit together. Your knee is probably fine and I'm not going to let you ruin the rest of this trip.'

I grumbled for a few hours about catching a ferry to Athens in search of a decent Lachman tester, but Justine's talking sorted me out. By that night I was back on planet earth, tucking into another Greek salad.

A week later I was back at the football club. Our surgeon, David Young, came in to give me a routine check-up and laid me down on the doctor's table for 'the test'.

I'd be lying if I said that I wasn't worried, but as expected David locked the knee out and there was an endpoint that felt as solid as a dead bolt.

I won't lie: it was nice to get a proper Lachman.

Sunday, 10 April 2016: Western Bulldogs v. Hawthorn, Etihad Stadium

A Hawthorn player roosts the ball into play from the kick-in. It's an attempted torpedo punt that doesn't come off the boot sweetly, tumbling awkwardly up the middle of the ground towards the outstretched hands of a mob of players. This is a critical contest and there's a sense of desperation in the air. The Bulldogs are on top of the ladder, undefeated, and three points in front with 90 seconds to go – against perhaps the greatest team of all. It's only round three of the season, but it feels significant. Just two years ago, this team and my club were spoken of as being insignificant. Now we're playing in the match of the round and it's been a classic. The ship has turned for good.

The ball hits hands and falls to the ground, and although the Bulldogs have the numbers, the Hawks win the important possession, shuffling the ball out to one of their stars, Shaun Burgoyne. Ordinarily, Shaun's a player with all the time in the world when he has the ball in his hands, but he's not sure how long is left, so he kicks the ball hard and straight towards goal.

I'm one-on-one with another of their stars, Luke Breust, just inside their 50-metre line. I know this will be the moment that will decide the game, and I get a rush of excitement and energy. I position myself between Breust and the ball, but as I turn to push him in the chest and make a play on the ball, I'm confronted by someone else. James Sicily has (to me, at least) popped up out of nowhere, and I know we're now in real trouble. With all my might, I try to pivot on my left foot to get across to spoil him and save the day, but as my foot plants in the turf and I put all my power through the leg, I hear the crunch of bone and the pop of my anterior cruciate ligament. It's like the sound a grape makes if you squeeze it between your fingertips.

Straight away, I know my knee's gone.

There's no doubt in my mind.

I'm not conscious of any physical pain. Sicily has marked the ball, of course, and is lining up to put his side in front, but I've travelled sideways into another world, a grim, colourless place. The trainers are quickly by my side and as our physio, Chris Bell, runs towards me, someone asks, 'What have you done?'

With a sense of resignation, I say, 'It's gone.'

With Bulldogs trainers Dale and Frank each holding me under one arm, I'm half-carried half-walked off the field, and I go into a la-la land kind of shock. My mind quickly races ahead to confirming the rupture of my ACL and what that means. A quick stocktake establishes that:

1. I've done my knee; my season is gone.
2. I've done my knee; my career is over.
3. I won't be a part of a Bulldog premiership.
4. This is my last moment on a footy field.

At this point it all becomes a bit too much. I can't take it in and I'm almost certainly in a state of shock. The feeling is like the spinning rainbow wheel of death, that thing your computer does when it hasn't got the capacity to keep up with what you're demanding of it.

Not quite frozen, but pretty close. I'm a spinning rainbow wheel.

I barely register the thunderous roar of the crowd behind me, but I grasp just enough to compute that Sicily has kicked the goal and won the game.

We lose.

I'm done for.

What a fucking cruel game.

I get to the bench and see Garry Zimmerman and I know what's about to happen and it sickens me. 'Zimmer' leads me straight down to the rooms for the test, just as he did ten years ago at the MCG. As we walk towards the doctors' private room, Justine is coming the other way and she just looks so damn sad. We adjourn into Zimmer's room, where he starts to bend and twist my knee around, and for a few moments there is a sense of optimism among the onlookers that I may have just strained my medial ligament. That would mean six to ten weeks on the sidelines, but I know in my heart that it's much, much worse.

For a start, when Zimmer tests the ACL he asks me to relax my leg, otherwise the test can be unreliable. Try as I might, I can't even relax my backside! Every ounce of my body is rigid like a plank of wood. I'm trying to stay strong, trying to delay what I know is about to come. I've done my knee, its insides are ripped apart. A few minutes later as the shock eases and I start to let go, David Young arrives. He holds my left leg in his hands and I can feel the knee joint is unstable. He goes through the motions and lets out a sigh. The ligament has completely ruptured.

The enormity of it all starts to hit home. The rainbow wheel has gone now and the tears start to roll. Justine holds onto me as I stare at the roof and cry for the first of many times.

A few players and staff enter the room to put their hand on my chest, including Clay Smith, who is recovering from a third knee reconstruction himself. He looks shattered. But for the most part it's just Justine and me, left alone to hold onto one another and brace ourselves for what we know is going to be a very bumpy road.

After a few minutes Luke Beveridge comes in. Without a word, he puts his arms around us both. It's funny how some people elicit such an emotional response from you, and that's how I am with Luke. He has been the coach I always wanted to have and such a big part of the reason I'm still playing and playing well. I want to play for *him*. I'm now sobbing tears at the realisation that that is gone too. I will never get to play for him again. It breaks me into a thousand pieces.

As we all hold on tight, Luke asks, 'Can you come back from this?'

I don't say a word.

11

The Apprenticeship

A journalist once asked me about the significance of joining the player leadership group, and how I found out I was in the group. I couldn't resist. 'Well, once the votes had been cast, a plume of white smoke was sent skyward out the top of the chimney …' My tip of the hat to the Vatican protocol for the announcement of a new Pope got full marks from my former-nun mother when it made the evening news.

Leadership in football is too broad to capture in a neat package. My view on what fits under the banner of leadership has changed a lot over the years. I've been a bit like a magpie building a nest – I've pinched bits of this and bits of that. By nature I'm an observer, and I absorb things that appeal to me. They say good artists borrow and great ones steal. I think the same could be said of leadership. For the kids out there, steal the bits you like! As a young player, I was pegged as a 'future leader', but if I'm honest I never really saw my destiny as a footballer ending with the captaincy of the Bulldogs. It's also worth noting that the term 'future leader' is sometimes applied to any young footballer with athletic talent and an ability to execute fully formed sentences.

It was never a conscious thought at the time, but the leaders of the Western Bulldogs in my formative years seemed too far out of reach for a skinny kid from Warragul. I was a bit of a dreamer, prone to bouts of stargazing, laziness and time-management-induced crises on a daily basis. Our leaders had their shit together, basically, and I didn't. We had football in common and that was about it. From the top down, I couldn't see much of myself in any of the football club's leaders.

David Smorgon was our president from 1997 until 2013, and his presence cast a big shadow over Whitten Oval. David was a very visible president, who always spoke with great passion and optimism, which I'm sure wasn't always easy during those long years. I can still remember his withering look when I arrived at a club media announcement wearing thongs.

As is often the way with young people, I was a little intimidated by Smorgo in those early years. This was more a function of my own insecurity than it is a criticism of David. It can't have been an easy job to lead the Bulldogs through that era. He was always eager, to the point of being impatient, for our young players to explore their leadership potential. I regret not pursuing it with him more at the time.

Terry Wallace was a coach with a razor-sharp eye on the game and his players. I frustrated most of my early coaches with my lack of intensity, and Plough let me have it on more than a few occasions. Even now, if I hear his voice on TV or radio, I get a little shiver. 'Murph, you were assassinated tonight!' Not once did I feel hard done by though. Like a wild brumby, I needed to be broken in, and Plough did much of the early legwork. I was still only very young when he left in dramatic circumstances near the end of 2002, and I don't feel like we ever quite really connected. I thought we would have more time together – I just assumed he would be around as senior coach for many years to come.

In the locker room, we had a shy and dignified captain in Chris Grant, someone we all looked up to like he was some sort of prophet. He probably is. It's not that I couldn't connect with Chris, but how do you see your likeness in another if that other is from the football heavens?

Underneath the skipper were a couple of hardened, professional deputies in Scott West and Luke Darcy. These two were ruthless competitors, hard trainers who wore the cloak of confrontation a lot easier than most. I'm sure my laissez-faire façade frustrated them at times, especially Westy. Luke and I are close; I always admired him for his conviction as much as anything. There's not much grey area with Darce, at least there wasn't back then. I loved playing under him when he became captain in 2005. I don't think I was like him, but I admired so much about him, especially during those early years. He knew when to put his arm around me and when I needed some home truths.

Brad Johnson and Rohan Smith were the other two lieutenants during this period and they were both pretty close to how you might imagine them. More 'bright spaces' than 'dark places'. Johnno and Smithy were the living embodiment of the Australian dream. Best mates, with beautiful wives and kids, living in the peaceful beachside suburb of Williamstown, playing footy on the weekend for the club they both grew up barracking for. No wonder they were always smiling.

But as a young man, I saw that tranquillity and pace of life as too slow for my gypsy heart. I wanted ripped jeans, op shops, best on grounds, boozy weekends, Fitzroy coffee shops, and *Exile on Main St*. I wanted too much. On the football field, I wanted to be the second coming of Bulldogs and Tigers gun Leon Cameron, kicking on both sides of my body and gliding across the flanks with graceful ease. Off the field, despite looking like the awkward work experience kid with acne, I wanted to be the lovechild of Huckleberry Finn and Stevie Nicks. I wanted to soak up this big city that seemed so new and exciting. I wanted adventure.

These men I've mentioned are some of the greatest leaders and characters in our club's history, but they were also very orthodox. The leadership poster boy of the competition around this time was Michael Voss, the triple premiership captain of the Brisbane Lions. I think that in itself encapsulates the times and culture of the game then – football was a far more male-dominated, macho beast at the turn of the millennium than it is today. Players are different now: they play just as hard as in any era, but they are more courageous in showing their emotions and more willing to empathise with teammates who show theirs.

At that time in my life, I was anything but orthodox. Depending on what day it was, I might have been described as 'quirky' or maybe even 'a bit loose'. The AFL is a pretty conservative environment with many rules. When most people leave school, they experience a sudden burst of freedom – you're out in the world, headed for the big cities or the open road, with a suitcase and a Tom Petty album blaring out of the speakers. But I got drafted, so I went straight into the conservative world of AFL. Playing was my dream, but there was an internal tug of war between that dream and the lure of late-teenage adventure.

There was a brief time early in my career when I didn't even have a training bag to carry my gear in. I'd rock up to the club with my boots and shorts, singlet and towel under my arm. I only remember this because a few of these orthodox grown-ups would laugh and shake their heads at me. Eventually Darce had a quiet word, suggesting I 'tidy up my professionalism'. I'm embarrassed at the memory of it now, but that's how happy-go-lucky I could be. It's no wonder I felt being a leader at an AFL club was a bit out of my reach.

I'm still in awe of those guys I've mentioned in lots of ways, but in recent years I've wondered if I might have picked up the leadership bug sooner if I'd played more than one season under the captaincy of Scott Wynd. But even just one year and three senior games under Wyndy was enough for his style to leave a big impression on me. He had a way about him that I connected with straight away.

In my first senior game, against Carlton at Princes Park, Wyndy called the boys into a tight huddle just before the first bounce. It's easy to feel lost and alone in the jungle of the AFL when you're starting out. I was nervous, as you'd expect, but his words calmed me. Wyndy told us a story. In his firm but gentle manner, 'The Gipper', as he was affectionately known, wondered aloud: 'What will it be like, one day, 15 years from now, when we bump into each other on the street? We'll talk about this day, the day we took on Carlton and beat them with a bunch of young kids on their home ground.' It was stirring stuff. The day needed something different to the normal approach and Wyndy must have known it. Good leaders recognise those moments. Great leaders know when to intervene and when to let things flow.

That day, the Bulldogs were rank underdogs and Carlton were rampaging, on a 13-game winning streak. The week before, they'd beaten Collingwood by 111 points. I can still close my eyes and feel what it was like to be in that scrum of players, the brotherhood it spoke to. I can hear the words of our skipper, but it's Wyndy's use of silence that's stayed with me the most. When Wyndy talks, he speaks softly and often lets the words hang in the air for a moment longer than you're expecting. It takes confidence to tell stories like that and to hold an audience. Three games and one season just weren't enough. On that sunny day, we beat Carlton by three points. And yes, we bump into each other and still talk about it. It was a perfect football day and it was my first. It doesn't get much better than that.

After adjusting to life as a professional footballer in those first few years, I began to build a career on the half-back flank for the Bulldogs and quickly found myself in the player leadership group. But my ambition was more tied to my status as a player than a yearning for the top job. I was really proud to be in that group – it was an acknowledgement from my club and peers that I was a good footballer, but was I a leader yet? Probably not. Daniel Giansiracusa and I were in the leadership group as an investment of sorts, a nod to the future. I wanted to help the team and influence the club, and there was a part of me that liked the status too. If I was in the leadership group that meant I was a bona fide league footballer.

Hindsight is a wonderful thing, and I reminisce on this time in my football life with a nagging frustration that I didn't wake up a bit earlier. My ambition as a kid had always been to play AFL – whether that was one game or 200 was really up to the gods. Being seen as a leader hadn't interested me much because I was too immature and self-centred to really think about what it *could* be. I toiled away on the half-back flank for quite a few years before the leadership pennies started to drop.

A chat one day with one of my childhood heroes and a Bulldogs assistant coach at the time, Wayne Campbell, changed my life. After a Saturday morning run around The Tan, we walked for a little while to mull over football and life. Wayne is one of my favourite people I've met in footy – a logical thinker, someone who's interesting and interested. Over the years our conversations have been long and can wind up in all sorts of places. Quite often they turn into a debate, which I always enjoy, because that's how discussions usually went around our kitchen table when I was growing up. It's quite a thing to grow up with someone as your hero and then for that person to become a friend.

But back on the Tan running track around the beautiful botanical gardens, we were player and coach. As we walked and talked, I think Wayne sensed some unease in me, that perhaps I wasn't as fulfilled with football or my place in it as I could be. On this day there was no debate, we were just shooting the breeze.

I voiced some concern that so much of what I was told about leadership in footy seemed to be about following rules. I understood that putting the work in and living a life of discipline was a big part of setting a good example and influencing things, but I suppose I wanted to explore rather than just stick to the formulaic approach that was the norm at the time.

Wayne told me, 'You know, there's enormous power in showing vulnerability. And *that* is leadership too.'

It was as if a door that had been jammed shut for years had opened and I was able to step through it. I felt like Wayne understood and could help guide me to a place that balanced the two sides of the coin: the need to be tough, disciplined and maybe even ruthless, with the other side of tenderness, conversation and the courage to be vulnerable in front of your peers. That's when I became intrigued about what being a leader could be.

As they say, it's better late than never.

Monday, 11 April 2016: Northcote

I've been sitting on the couch all night drinking wine until I'm fuzzy in the head. My knee is swollen but I'm not in much pain. My mate Denis Bicer, our club media manager, sits on the floor next to Peter Gordon and his wife Kerri, Jordan Roughead and his girlfriend Bridget Davies, and Easton Wood. Justine bustles about playing host, distracting herself from our new plight.

The proper sadness hasn't kicked in. Yet. But the vibe is still pretty heavy. My season is done and I feel like my playing days are over, but there's no hurry to make that call apparently. Easton is the skipper now. It hurts to let it go, but as far as deputies go he's right off the top shelf.

Easton seems just as shocked about my football mortality teetering on the edge as I am. He's an emotional boy. I love him. In a rare sober moment, I told him he shouldn't now try to be anything new. If he does that, the boys will smell it a mile away. I told him to just be himself and they'll follow him to the moon.

Tomorrow I have to get a scan on my knee and meet with David Young about surgery. It's all a formality, but no doubt I'll have to do the dance in front of the media too. That's all part of the show, but I don't want to be around people. I want oblivion.

Gerard Whateley says sport is the dessert trolley of life, and I think that sums it up pretty well. I've done my knee, no-one has died. But it still feels like grief.

It's quite late when everyone leaves to go home, but despite all the wine I can't find the sanctuary of slumber. Over and over in my head I can hear and feel the noise of my knee injury. *Crunch, twist-pop! Crunch, twist-pop! Crunch, twist-pop!* It's almost sunrise when I finally fall asleep.

12

The Hot Seat

Football is tough. There was a quote doing the rounds in our locker room a few years ago from Michael Tuck, a 426-game, seven-time premiership player and six-season club captain. The quote was never verified, but I won't forget it. 'Football is an endless parade of kicks in the guts.' Michael Tuck said that?! The man played so many games you'd have to assume he was never seriously injured, and his seven premierships speak to a gluttony of on-field success. It made me wonder: if the game was that tough on Michael Tuck, what hope is there for the rest of us?

You need armour to protect yourself in footy. A lot of that armour is physical – we train our bodies to withstand the hits and bumps over the long summers and bitter winters. But our minds also harden over time, like saddle leather, until so many seasons have passed we're almost unrecognisable. Innocent boys became battle-weary men.

The vulnerability Wayne Campbell opened my eyes to on that walk around The Tan was not something I'd ever heard discussed.

Weakness – or any of its cousins – was to be suppressed and ignored. Let's not forget St Kilda's Max Hudghton attempting to wash away his tears with water from a drink bottle after a particularly painful loss. This had been the culture in the macho, male-dominated sport for more than a century. To hear Cambo, one of my heroes, use the word 'vulnerability' and speak of its untapped potential seduced me, because I knew I could use it.

I think what's relevant here is the age of professionalism in football. For 100 years, Australian Rules was an amateur sport, with training a couple of nights a week and a game on the weekend. During the mid-1990s, the game and its players moved to a professional model, where players train, meet, educate and recover from the rigours of the game five to six days a week during business hours. That was a huge cultural leap in terms of time spent together in the pack. Whenever this transition in football from amateur to professional is discussed, the focus quickly becomes the huge increase in wages. But I think the amount of time players spend together has been just as significant in changing the culture. A coach berating you in traditional fire-and-brimstone fashion was a lot easier to take when you only saw that coach for six hours a week. It's a different story when you spend 40 hours a week with your coaches and teammates, trying to push each other along in the hope of winning games of footy.

Consequently, in the professional landscape of AFL, different models of leadership have become very significant. From 2008 to 2010, the Bulldogs made the fashionable transition to the Leading

Teams model of leadership facilitation. At the time, Leading Teams was very popular among AFL teams, on the back of the premiership success enjoyed by Geelong and Sydney. Through this player-driven model, the Swans adopted a subculture, styling themselves 'The Bloods'. I was envious of them, and I'm sure I wasn't the only league footballer at the time who felt a little jealous of this mythical Bloods culture.

Under the Leading Teams model, a facilitator comes in to work with the players and the focus for the early meetings is perceptions: how the rest of the competition perceives the group, and how the group wants to be perceived. Through that process, some keywords, or themes, are fleshed out until a few values emerge: these will become your club's 'trademark'. A mission statement of sorts. At the Bulldogs during those three years, our trademark was:

Consistent

Ruthless

United

(Our team voted on a theme to cover our trademark. I offered up 'Sons of the West' because I thought it captured the link between our past players and the future, but I lost the vote to an acronym. CRU. I've never gotten over it.)

It all sounds a bit quaint now, but at the time it felt quite revolutionary. Leading Teams became controversial in the ensuing years, mostly due to the practice of peer assessments. In a peer assessment, if you're in the 'hot seat', you're given a sheet of paper and asked to leave the room. Your teammates then gather in groups of five or six, each with the same piece of paper you have. Once outside, your job is to predict how the rest of the group will describe you. From top to bottom the sheet reads:

What three words would you like the group to describe you with?

How would the group describe you in three words?

What does the group want you to STOP doing?

What does the group want you to START doing?

What does the group want you to KEEP doing?

After the first few players are peer-assessed, it quickly becomes routine, but no-one forgets the first time they're asked to leave the room. I remember being quite anxious; finding out what your peers really think about you is daunting, but the physicality of it also caught me off-guard. I had to actually get up out of my seat and leave the room. I'd spent my whole life inside sporting teams, and for a few minutes I was outside the safety of the pack while my teammates dissected my football soul. It's a long way out of your comfort zone for even the hardest professional. I remember our facilitator at the time telling us that 'eventually you will look forward to being peer-assessed, you may even crave it'. At the time, I could not imagine a world where that would be the case, but he proved to be right. My first peer assessment was not nearly as confronting as I thought it might be. I was pleased that the players acknowledged how hard I ran on the field to offer a lead for my teammates, but there was a general sense that my feedback to teammates during a game was a bit too harsh. Curiously, one of the groups used the word 'alternate' to describe me. I can only assume they meant 'alternative'. No surprise there.

Leading Teams became infamous because of peer assessments that became confrontational. Famously, at Geelong, Gary Ablett Jr's teammates told him they didn't think he trained hard enough and wasn't getting the best out of himself. But 95 per cent of the peer assessments I witnessed over three years weren't nearly as memorable as that. Most of the time, the players' predictions and the group's assessment were very close and often, if the player was surprised, it was because the group was quite complimentary towards them and they'd prepared themselves for something with more teeth. But those few occasions where things went off-course were quite tense, it has to be said.

This was the era when the Jason Akermanis show came to town at our club. Jason was an exquisitely talented footballer who had won a Brownlow medal and three premierships with the Brisbane Lions. But despite all of that success, he had fallen out with his teammates and his coach and was moved on. The Bulldogs signed him up at the end of 2007.

A founding principle of the Leading Teams model is the notion 'this is what the group wants from you to improve yourself and the team, and this is a plan to help you get there'. When the group asks you to change certain behaviours, that's what you set your mind and energy to do. It was very clear and direct. Jason was the only player who at times appeared not to accept what the group wanted. To me, he seemed to dispute or sometimes completely dismiss anything that was even remotely negative about his application as a footballer. I was one of several players who was offended by this reluctance to listen to the feedback and get on with it.

After lengthy discussions, the group decided that Jason's much-talked-about victory handstand was not in line with our new unified approach to all things 'team', and you can imagine how that went down. It's fair to say that we were quite militant as a group at the time. We believed we needed a hard-nosed approach to be the best. It may have been too hard at times, for sure, but that's how it was and we all had to adjust. We wanted a flag desperately.

The strain of the struggle between Jason and the wider group took a toll on everyone, but I was the focal point for a lot of his bitterness. Jason and I just didn't get on. Football only played a very small part in our fractured relationship. I can't think of anything that we agreed on: from politics to pop music, we were north and south poles.

I can be quick to judge, too quick at times, and I've been accused of having an acidic tongue. On a pre-season camp down at Wilson's Promontory, not long after Jason had arrived at the club, we had a talent show and Jason performed a stand-up routine. He bombed. No laughs. Afterwards in the common room, in front of a few people, I made a comment about how bad it had been. It cut him deeply. I regret that. Yes, I can be a prick.

Jason and I got off on the wrong foot and I never really tried to patch it up. One day we had a heated argument on the training track and our forward line coach, Wayne Campbell, sent us off to have lunch together to sort it out. It was a good move in theory, but when we sat down to eat the first thing that came out of his mouth was, 'Listen, I'm one of the great self-assessors.' It was a short lunch.

I didn't feel like Jason's motives at the Bulldogs were completely sincere. He played some great football for the Bulldogs, but I think he craved celebrity as much as anything. For a time, the city of Melbourne gave him that exalted status. Could I have handled the situation better at the time? Yes. I could have tried harder and been more patient. But I wasn't captain at the time and he was the elder of us. I don't feel it should have fallen to me and others to convince him of what the team wanted from him time and time again. It was exhausting.

Eventually the club terminated his contract and he was shown the door. An accumulation of things brought a messy situation to that point. Jason wrote an article for the *Herald Sun* that ran under the headline 'Gay Footballers, Stay in the Closet'. In it, he wrote that the world of AFL was 'not ready' for a player to come out and that it would 'cause discomfort'. Jason had initially wanted to write a piece on homosexuality in sport with the help of Pippa Grange at the AFL Players Association. After offering her help, Pippa was shocked and horrified by what ended up in the paper. Unsurprisingly, the article created a media storm and Jason then had the gall to sit in front of our leadership group and complain about the backlash he'd received.

I tried to explain to him by saying, 'When you write that stuff, the rest of us have to defend you in the media.'

He looked so confused. 'Yeah, but I'm getting smashed by people out there.'

'You wrote the article!' I snapped back. But it was useless.

At that point, I didn't think he was capable of thinking about his effect on the club and I gave up on him. Once word filtered through to our captain, Brad Johnson, not long after this that Jason was writing his second explosive autobiography and planned to take down a few of his teammates (including me) in it, things escalated quickly and he was gone. The club had had enough of the damage he was doing in the locker room. Football clubs are very forgiving places, and this was the second club to ask him to leave and take his undeniable talents with him. I think that says a lot.

The media interest around homophobia in sport, specifically football, comes and goes like the tide. Jason's article was offensive on a number of levels and it cut me deeply. I can only imagine how it must have felt for a homosexual footballer or for the broader gay community.

A couple of years after Jason's departure I had to front the media for a standard press conference after training. The only reason I was out front was because I was rostered on. The day before, Jeff Kennett had made headlines by proclaiming that up to 5 per cent of footballers must be gay (roughly two or three at each club). I was asked about Jeff's comments.

'I think there's a bit of a sick fascination I hear from people on the street about who it is and how many there are,' I said. 'I think that's really irrelevant. It's about an environment of accepting not just people who are gay, but from all walks of life and different outlooks on things. The culture of footy now is one that's very accepting. This club's one of great acceptance.'

What wasn't reported, as far as I know, was the answer I gave to one of the journalists, who, to my eye, wasn't a sports journalist. She asked loaded questions about the nasty culture within football clubs that has prevented an AFL player from coming out. Mind you, at the time we were still years away from our own government giving same-sex couples the opportunity to marry. And it's the fault of football clubs? Please.

I said I could only speak for my own club, but that I couldn't imagine it being a big deal for players. I thought the prospect of media intrusion was probably a bigger deterrent in stopping players from coming out.

I've tried to imagine myself as a gay footballer and how my life would change if I came out publicly as a gay man. It would be front- and back-page news, probably for more than just that day. Potentially I would be cast as the spokesperson for all gay footballers – on any number of political issues, whether I wanted to be or not. My private life would be the intrigue of the football and broader media, and I would open myself up to public criticism, particularly in the murky waters of social media.

Most footballers just want to play. They don't want any extra attention. They don't want to be the spokesperson for anything. Being judged for the way they play the game alone is enough to cause most players at least some level of anxiety. In light of that, the first AFL player to come out as a gay man deserves all the plaudits that will come his way from the right kind of people. It will take courage. Real courage. The first one through that wall will have my utmost respect, as will those who choose to follow his lead. I know in my heart that modern footballers will embrace them with love and kindness. I'm not sure I have the same confidence in some sections of the modern media.

There was one other thing the Leading Teams format made me reflect on during the time we used it at the club: that because of the 5 per cent of times it goes off-course, its reputation is damaged, which saddens me a little. My experience of the program was that it was an education in showing vulnerability as much as anything. For those three years, all of our other sessions at the club (as full-time footballers) were about putting the armour on (weights, boxing, skills, rehab). Those CRU meetings were about taking all that heavy steel off. Wayne was right – there was enormous power in laying it all out there.

In the end, though, the weekly meetings took their toll on everybody. The fanatics (which now included myself) stayed engaged and tried to drive the group further and further, but it was a heavy load to carry for those who weren't as interested in the meetings. I had to admit that after three years of intense introspection the 'no humour' policy had run its race. There's a constant balance in AFL footy of keeping things light and fun while maintaining a razor-sharp focus on what's at stake and what it takes to achieve your aims. Our three years with the CRU burned us all out.

Sunday, 29 May 2016: Palm Springs, California

I've got the California blues. Just as we did ten years ago when I injured my knee, Justine and I have slipped out of town to clear our heads and decide whether or not I have it in me to play football again. We got on a plane, spent a couple of days visiting friends in San Diego and then drove out to Palm Springs to ponder the future. Maybe the desert has some answers: just as it had for my folks and Jesus before me.

Right now, I'm sitting by the pool with Justine at the Parker Hotel in Palm Springs under a scorching sun. They're playing sweet pop tunes from speakers behind the palm trees. Pacifico, the great Mexican beer, is on tap and the staff are generous enough to take our order for 'two more' and deliver them to our sun beds.

The Parker may be the best hotel we've ever been to in our lives. It looks like a pool party at Frank Sinatra's house in 1958.

So why have I got the blues? The idea of this getaway was to disappear for ten days and clear my thoughts. It's been an exhausting few weeks back home dealing with the injury. But it doesn't matter how far you run sometimes, you can never outrun your own shadow.

Back home, the Bulldogs are playing the Magpies at the MCG and that's where I should be. I can feel it in my stomach. They still feel like my team. This feeling is the strongest sign yet that maybe I've got a bit more in the tank. I suppose that's a good thing, a glorious thing even.

So, maybe it's not the blues, maybe it's the engines rumbling again.

13

Bottoming Out

From 2008 to 2010, the Bulldogs made the preliminary final each year. In 2011, the team's winning form fell apart and we crashed out of the finals, costing Rodney Eade his job. Brendan McCartney took over, and the first 18 months of his tenure were great. Brendan took us back to school. I often referred to the football education sessions during this time as 'football TAFE'. Brendan brought a much more structured football program and game style than we'd previously had under Rocket.

Hindsight is a wonderful thing, but on the football style spectrum I don't think you could get a bigger discrepancy than the Eade Bulldogs of 2004 to 2011 compared to the McCartney Bulldogs of 2012 to 2014. Under Rocket, we had a game style that encouraged offence. We were a diagonal kicking team that took great delight in running fast, bouncing the ball as we went. When Brendan came on board, he wanted to slow things down, get more numbers around the contest and get bigger bodies in the middle of the ground.

Actually, he wanted bigger bodies all over the ground. The game style had a much greater emphasis on defence and contested ball. We embarked on a leg weights program that was so intense that Lindsay Gilbee ripped his wedding suit under the strain of his 'new' backside in the first pre-season of the McCartney years. It might be that the drastic change in game styles was just too big a bridge to get over for our playing group. It never really clicked on the field.

By the end of Brendan's second year at the helm, and with a couple of losing seasons under our belt, the pressure rose and so did the underflow of discontent among the players. Brendan often used the phrase 'the old Bulldogs' and it didn't go down well with a few players. I wasn't happy about it. On the training track, he would sometimes bark instructions about the style of footy he wanted, adding for emphasis, 'We are not going to play like the old Bulldogs.' The inference (as I took it) was that we had played offensive, bruise-free footy and now we were going to play men's footy. Geelong footy. Footy that actually won finals.

We're a pretty sensitive bunch, us footballers, especially when it comes to our legacy. One day, on a sunbaked Whitten Oval, I'd just had enough. I stopped training momentarily and looked at Macca for a long time, visibly pissed off. 'Don't look at me like that, Robert,' he said with a smile. I put my head back down, finished the day's training and went home.

Macca called on the Sunday, but I was still seething, so I waited until Monday to talk it out. To his credit, he heard me out, and I don't remember Brendan ever using 'the old Bulldogs' line again after our chat. I tried to explain to him that while he may be right in the long run, those years might have been the last shot for some of us, and despite falling short we were proud of what we had achieved. I had a bumpy road with Macca, but we were able to work our way through it. Others weren't.

The 2014 season was a torrid one for everyone associated with the club. We finished 14th, winning a miserable seven games. And that was on the back of two losing seasons. I can't overemphasise the pressure that builds inside a club after three losing seasons in a row.

In the final game for 2014, the Bulldogs went down dramatically to a GWS side that we should have beaten. It was Daniel Giansiracusa's last game for the club and he deserved a lot more than what we served up that day. I've had some bad days in footy and endured some pretty depressing post-match meetings, but this was the big daddy of them all.

Brendan stood in front of us, hands in his pockets, and kept repeating, 'I'm not sure what you want me to say, I'm not sure what you want me to do.' This was not just in front of the players, but most of the inner sanctum of the club as well. My instincts told me that not only were we a team in real trouble, but Brendan as coach was in grave trouble too. He looked like a man who had taught us all he knew and didn't know what to do next. There was a feeling of hopelessness in the room, and then it was over. There was no bright note or glimpse of sunshine to tuck into our pockets for the next pre-season, just a few details about where we should meet to drown our sorrows and toast one of the club's greats.

A week or two passed, nothing happened, and I assumed things had been resolved behind closed doors and that it would be business as usual when pre-season started. I headed off on a family holiday to Bali with Justine and our three kids.

I was on a beach when the first signs of the earthquake that was to hit the club appeared. With water gently lapping at my feet and the heat of the sun offset by a cold beer, I leaned across to grab my phone and check my emails. There was an email from the club with the subject 'Urgent'. The first line read, 'Ryan Griffen's management has informed us …'

That was all my iPhone would let me read because the wifi cut out, but I could join the dots from there. I made a call back home and got confirmation of what had happened. Eventually my internet coverage returned and I read all of the reports on Twitter. In a trade week bombshell, our captain, Ryan Griffen, had announced his immediate departure from the club, seeking a trade to the GWS Giants.

I was absolutely stunned. I know I wasn't alone. The aftershocks of this quake in Australia could be felt all the way to my Indonesian paradise and beyond; players were scattered all around the world on their holidays. Griff was a reluctant captain, a shy kind of guy who was far and away our best player. The added responsibility never seemed to sit comfortably on his shoulders and although I wasn't in the leadership meetings in 2014, I got the feeling they had become tense and quite possibly toxic. There was a disconnect between the players and Macca, obviously, but it was hard to see how it could be repaired now. Instinctively, I knew that if the captain left like this, the coach would be likely to follow him. Whether he resigned or was sacked, I couldn't imagine how he could come back from this. Sure enough, Macca resigned as senior coach a few days later.

We were a club in crisis, there was no doubt about that. I felt a deep sense of disappointment and shame. As the oldest player, I had to take responsibility, I spent the rest of my holiday doing a bit of soul-searching. Did I do enough? Have I let the club down? What do we do now? But even in those dramatic minutes on that beach as I tried to digest all the information, my thoughts went to the captaincy. I needed to step up to the plate. In the days and weeks that followed, I thought of little else other than how to get our club back on track. It was time for all hands on deck.

Thursday, 14 July 2016: Whitten Oval

After we got back from Palm Springs, I announced that I would play on again in 2017 and threw myself into my knee rehabilitation. I stepped up my duties as the off-field captain too. I would meet regularly with the coach, footy manager and player welfare officer to gauge the temperature of the group. It felt good to keep busy and protect the energy levels of my deputies in the leadership group by shielding them from even more meetings. Everything was moving smoothly. And then we hit a snag.

It started with a rather puzzling cut under the eye of Zaine Cordy when he fronted for training. Some pointed questions were asked of him by management and the player leaders. It soon became apparent that something more sinister had gone down last weekend. A second party is involved. Tom Boyd. Tom hit Zaine when they were out drinking.

I've spoken with both boys and I'm still a little unclear about what really happened. It seems Zaine poured some of his drink down Tom's back when he was doing his shoelace and Tom got up and clocked him. In some ways, the exact details don't matter. What is important is that our big-name recruit and full forward has lost the trust of the group as a result of whacking a teammate.

Inevitably, the media has found out about it, and the whole thing is all over the TV and in the newspapers, just as we knew it would be. I'm not nearly as worried about that as I am about steering the team's ship to calmer waters.

With the very best of intentions, Bevo has dropped the conundrum in the lap of the player leaders. 'When Tom has the trust of the playing group, he will be available for selection,' he said as both players were suspended indefinitely. It sounded good at the time.

The last few weeks have been difficult, certainly the most difficult of my captaincy. The ambiguity around 'trust of the playing group' has cornered us. Is it unanimous? Majority? The truth is that a handful of players aren't yet comfortable with the trust factor. A player punching a teammate could take months, not games, to recover from.

I can understand the hurt. Players occasionally get narky with each other, but throwing a proper punch at a teammate on the weekend is serious. Maybe in years gone by this kind of thing happened with less fuss, but not nowadays. The fact that it's Tom just makes the whole drama even more significant. He's only been with us for 18 months, and he hasn't yet proven himself on the field, not consistently anyway. There's not that much 'water in the well', as the saying goes. And, of course, he's on a million dollars a season. It hadn't seemed an issue among our players before this, but it could be now. I'm not sure.

I have sympathy for both sides. I'm angry about Tom's actions, obviously, but I also see a young man under enormous pressure. A prodigious talent who has the unenviable weight of ridiculous external expectation on him. No 19-year-old in the history of the game has had to put up with as much online vitriol and constant critiquing as Tom has. Maybe some kind of lashing out was inevitable.

I like Tom, he's thoughtful and has a gentle heart, but he's a bit distant and can sometimes even seem a bit cold towards his teammates. We all have masks though, don't we?

All of the leaders are caught in the middle, but it's me in the hot seat. There's already enough tension among the playing group over this issue that I'm very conscious of the need to avoid creating a divide between the leadership group and a section of the playing group. This is my job as captain. I'm the classic middle man, in a sense, trying to counsel the group through all of this while balancing the coach's desires. Bevo wants Tom back in. He wants him back in immediately. I've locked the players in a room twice already, both times without Tom in the room. 'Are you ready for him to come back in?' I ask. Mostly they are, yes, but there are still a few determined nos. I'm worried about a lot of things, but the main thing is that I could hold a player vote for the next ten weeks and still not get a unanimous call of yes. No team can survive that kind of internal destruction.

A few of my teammates have accused me of playing to the coach's tune. At least, that's what's got back to me. It's the first time I've felt this level of loneliness in the job. Matty Boyd senses this and seeks me out almost daily to check how I'm coping. He's a man who's felt this loneliness, I reckon. It feels good to have his support – he's a good man to have in your corner when the bell sounds.

I seek solace in our club psychologist, Lisa Stevens, too, and she gives me the key to unlock the door. She says, 'It's okay to forgive the person, but not the action.' That chimes with me. I hope it will for the players.

At the risk of appearing an appeaser for the coach, I'm not going through another soul-destroying player vote. I'm going to make a final call on this. When we next meet to discuss Tom's fate, I'm going to tell them he will miss one more week and then he's available. The coach won't be happy and a few of the players might not be satisfied either, but that's the way it goes. It does occur to me that it's quite likely no-one will be happy. Great leadership!

In the movie *Thirteen Days*, starting Kevin Costner as Kenny O'Donnell, special assistant to President John F. Kennedy as they work their way through the Cuban missile crisis, there's a line that has always stuck in my mind. At one point, with seemingly no way out without significant damage to the prospect of peace or a popular government, O'Donnell says, 'We will just have to take our hits along the way.' That chimes with truth for me too.

So I front the players to deliver my 'captain's call', and throw up a Hail Mary. 'Unless we have a consensus, Tom will miss this week and be available to play next week. Is there consensus?' The mood in the room feels different. More empathy, somehow. More tenderness. There have been a lot of conversations going on these past few days about this issue. The leaders have all been trying hard to get Lisa's 'forgive the person' wisdom across. Maybe it's worked.

'Or are we happy for him to play this week?' Lots of heads are nodding, including heads from the previously disgruntled group. 'Right, it's sorted then. We can move on. He's back.' When you get the answer you want, end the conversation.

Big exhale.

JFK, I don't how you did it for 13 days, old boy.

Monday, 5 September 2016: Returning from the Pyrenees

I slipped back into my regular world this morning, arriving at Whitten Oval after having woken before dawn in the faraway Pyrenees ranges. There are grey skies overhead and I'm weary from the exertions of escape. Since I scurried off after training at lunchtime on Saturday, nobody here knows where I've been or how I've spent the weekend.

Our first final is looming, a trip over to Perth for a do-or-die game against the West Coast Eagles. It's Monday and the cogs are turning in the football department. There's an edge to the atmosphere, but for all intents and purposes it's business as usual. The players have had the weekend off and, my god, they look better for it.

It's a hot topic around town at the moment — for the first time, the eight teams good enough to make September have enjoyed a week's break before the finals. Nobody needed the rest more than my Bulldogs. We're banged up. Late last week, the boys had a training run, and the only way I can describe it is to use some football jargon. 'Shithouse' would be my summary. Forgive the technical speak.

Bevo and the match committee have taken the dramatic step of bringing in no fewer than five players for the West Coast game. I watch on in amazement as the boys train with a sparky zest. They look good. Actually, they look magnificent. Full of energy and spunk again. They're running on top of the ground, as the old adage goes. We're due for a bit of luck, it must be said. We've had a wretched run with injuries this year. West Coast might be in trouble, they just don't know it yet.

While my teammates rested their bodies at home on the weekend, I spent two days in the bush with a small group of mates: a motley crew of blokes that include an Italian osteopath, a Tasmanian bard, a broad-chested Northern Irish publican, a Fitzroy song-and-dance man and a left-hander from Birregurra. Our annual getaway usually falls in the first week of the finals.

This weekend at the end of my footy season has been been a bit of an anchor point for me these past five or six years. It's a chance to slip off the radar and wind down after the rollercoaster of another season of discipline and routine has ground to a halt. We call it camping, but nobody brings a tent. We rent a house in the hills, and the only real conditions are that it must have a fireplace, a fire pit and a view.

We sit around swapping stories and jokes with a drink in hand while the fire crackles away. Drunken speeches are sometimes made. In all of the years we've been camping, a cross word has never been uttered.

On our second camping trip some years back, we took turns standing on a fallen tree stump that lay near our bonfire to make a speech. The left-hander got up and said, 'It's important to occasionally turn off the lights. That's what camping is about.' It rang true with me. Sometimes we *do* need to turn off the lights. At least, that's how I feel at the end of every footy season.

This year I went away with my campers as usual, but in a sense I never really left home. I was distracted. I'm in a kind of football purgatory: neither inside my own team, nor completely out of it. Even up in the glorious hills, I couldn't disappear. I was restless.

With the fire roaring on Sunday night and the music getting louder, I crept to bed, sober, knowing I'd be up in the silent bush darkness to tackle the drive back to Footscray, to re-enter my other world. Neither a player, nor a camper. Among familiar faces, yet lost and alone.

Thursday, 29 September 2016: Whitten Oval, final training session

I've almost given up trying to work out how I feel this week. One moment I'm smiling broadly, the next I'm screaming inside at the injustice of it all.

The boys are in the grand final, the whole country seems to be buzzing with the romance of this unlikely footy team. There's a lot going on. Today was the last training session for the team before they take on the Swans at the MCG on Saturday. The big dance. It was pretty special to see 10,000 people at Whitten Oval for training, and the weather turned it on too.

Amid all of the drama going on from an emotional standpoint, I've had to endure the demands of rehabilitating after a knee reconstruction. I've been lucky to have Josh Prudden by my side the whole way. Josh did his knee in the reserves the week after I did mine against the Hawks back in April. We had our surgeries on the same day and have gone stride for stride trying to get healthy again.

I really admire Prudes – he's tough and determined. The game has been cruel to him and he keeps fronting up. I hope he gets a good run at it, because he deserves it and he's a damn good player when he's fit. Smart and creative. I like players like that. We've been blessed to have the best in the business as our 'rehab coach', Nick Stone. It's his job to put us through physical torture day after day and to motivate us and manage the psychology of a long rehabilitation. That's not easy. Not only does he do the job, but we love him for how much of himself he gives to us.

This week has been tough. All of the players who aren't playing are under a great deal of emotional strain, but we know we can't show it while we're at the club. It just wouldn't be fair on our 22 players. I invited the injured boys over for dinner on Monday night to make this point and to thank them for their efforts.

The fatigue of the arduous running sessions Prudes and I are doing keeps bringing my emotions to the surface. The boys are training, preparing for the biggest day in the club's history, and Prudes and I are running up and down the outer wing of the Whitten Oval with only a stopwatch for company. Absurdly, on Tuesday night, when the main group finished training, a few thousand supporters invaded the ground to kick their footballs. Josh and I still had two kilometres of running to complete. It was infuriating, dodging and weaving between euphoric supporters. At one point, a woman from Bendigo stopped in front of me to get a selfie and I nearly exploded. It was a farcical scene.

Today was a lot more orderly. Prudes and I were allowed to join in with the group for the warm-up kicking drills. We almost felt a part of things. But soon we had to return to our stopwatch routine. As we ran a few warm-up laps, the Bulldogs' supporters rose up to cheer us as we passed them. It was a lovely gesture that gave Prudes and I the giggles at first, but after our third lap of being cheered the whole way around the oval I wanted to scream 'Shut the fuck up!' Just let us be invisible now. Then I felt guilty for feeling like that.

These are my people and they are beaming with happiness. They are just so proud of their team. My frustration is not with them, it's with myself. I wish I felt the pure excitement that they all feel. I'm dying inside. Everyone has their limits and I feel like I'm not far away from a breakdown of some kind.

It's been such a long and draining year. I thought back today to a Tuesday night in July, the week after the Bulldogs had pinched a win from the Swans on the siren. I was split up from Prudes, doing some plyometric jump and land exercises on my own at the far end of the gym. Every other player was lifting weights at the other end of the room. After a few moments, I looked back at the group and realised I was standing under a blown light bulb, a lone figure swallowed up by its shadow. I was invisible to the group. It was a crushing metaphor for how this season has played out. I'm captain of this team, but I'm not in it. I'm the invisible man.

Back in the real world, with my sense of displacement elbowed to one side, it was utterly incredible to see all of those supporters back at the club for a grand final week training run. You can see what it means to them, just from the smiles on their faces. After training, all the boys gathered in the club's museum to eat lunch. I joined them, along with the great John Schultz. John will present the cup to Easton Wood if the Bulldogs can beat the Swans on Saturday.

John and I got chatting about the game, small-talk kind of stuff. Then he took my arm and said, 'When we win the premiership, make sure you stay near the dais because we want to get you involved.' I almost fainted hearing the word 'when'. There are certain rules in life, and one of those is you don't shush John Schultz. Having said that, I wanted to stuff a pair of socks down Shultzy's mouth. I didn't want the players to hear that kind of confidence. Or maybe I didn't want him to wake the ghosts of the past and jinx us.

Instead, I just looked at the floor and excused myself from lunch early.

Saturday, 1 October 2016: The MCG, Grand Final Day

I swallow a Valium capsule about five minutes before the team runs through the banner. The previous two hours have been passed shaking hands and hugging teammates and staff. Well wishes all round. I've almost mastered the art of keeping a calm façade while a panic attack bubbles under the surface like a giant Murray cod. The maniacal chewing of spearmint chewing gum is the only giveaway.

Cod aside, it feels good to be in the inner sanctum of the Bulldogs clan again. The waiting is almost over and I am with my people. We really have built a magnificent footy team on the foundations of a group of wonderful folk. I make my way around the rooms, speaking with each player, offering them what I can. But at this point of the season, less is more. Everyone knows what's at stake on Grand Final Day. Simply being in a room full of people is exhausting for me at the moment, and it's not long before I'm hiding in the toilets. Breathe slowly in. Slowly out.

Today will be a day like no other. A bit like the players, I'm under the microscope. I can feel eyes on me everywhere. At one point, I grab a football near the race and start to bounce it on the hallowed turf, heading for the middle of the MCG. After a few strides, I realise a television camera suspended in midair by wires is hovering a few feet over my head. I stand on the centre circle, bounce the ball to myself, turn, and walk back down the race. The camera follows me the whole way.

As Vika and Linda Bull put the finishing touches on the best national anthem heard at an AFL grand final in years, I'm chasing Bevo down through the interchange bench towards the lifts. It's just Luke, his security guard and me waiting for the lift doors to open. I look to our left, and standing about 30 metres away, playing the same waiting game, is Sydney coach John Longmire. It's a strange moment, each of us quiet and isolated, with the heaving madness of the stadium and the occasion above us.

A feeling comes over me that I really should have offered up my grand final ticket to someone else. With each final, I've progressively watched less and less of the game. The stress of the outcome is so excruciating that I spend a lot of time looking at the plastered ceiling seeking comfort. I barely watched last week's preliminary final against the Giants; it was just too tense.

My vantage point for Bulldogs games this year has been like a VIP ticket to a Bulldogs fantasy camp. I sit next to John Schultz and behind Chris Grant. John keeps a close eye on the ruckmen, watching their every move. Granty's level of stress can be recorded by his intake of lollies. He consumed a *lot* of lollies in Sydney last Saturday evening. In the moments after those crazy final minutes, with our first grand final berth in 65 years secured, Granty turned, grabbed me and whispered, 'We're there.' It summed up a lot and stirred the emotions in me.

As a club, we've been waiting for so long.

In those dying moments of the preliminary final, I was confronted with the likely possibility of missing out on the chance to play in a grand final. This critical juncture had been building for months and I had never been sure how I would feel if we actually made it. It's a terrible thing to lose control of your emotions, lose trust in your heart. I knew I'd be a jumbled mess, and I was terrified of not feeling any happiness in the event of victory and a grand final berth. What would this moment reveal?

But when the moment came – when the siren sounded and Granty whispered those words in my ear – I found a welcome perspective on how big this is for our footy club. And I got my answer about how I would feel watching the boys celebrate. I was happy. Granted, the happiness had a few warts on it, but I was relieved as much as anything. I was proud of the team and glad it was the Bulldogs who were there and not the Giants.

The opening minutes of any grand final are frenetic, but today seems turbo-charged. Players from both teams throw themselves into the congestion, causing plenty of spills and thrills. The early part of the game is low-scoring, which suits our camp just fine. The pattern of the Swans has been to blow teams out of the water early, before cantering home with a big lead. A focus in our preparation was to stay close to the Swans early.

After about 20 minutes, a high ball comes out of the centre square and floats into the Swans' attacking 50. Kieren Jack goes back with the flight, never taking his eyes off it. It's the type of situation every single player would have thought about as their head hit the pillow last night. 'If I'm in that situation, how will I react? Will I answer the challenge? Will I master the inherent fear? If I fail that test, can I handle the shame?'

Jack takes the mark, and Easton Wood is the train coming the other way. Woody hits him down the middle with a fierce shoulder, but his feet never leave the ground. It's an incredible moment of sporting bravery from both players, but particularly Jack. It's not so much a turning point, but a standard for the contest. This one is being played for all the marbles.

At quarter-time the Dogs have their noses in front. By the time I get down to the ground among the players, I can sense in their eyes the relief. Everywhere, I see a look that says, 'We haven't been blown out of the water.' It's almost as if the game can start, now that the business of being 'in the game' has been taken care of.

The tension never lets up. I twist my arms like a pretzel, trying to will the movement of the players or the ball psychosomatically from my comfy chair on level two. My fantasy camp is a mixed bag. Schultzy is very happy with Tom Boyd and Jordan Roughead's aerial dominance, while Granty is steadily picking up pace with the confectionary. By half-time I'm topping up my meds again.

Something that's struck me as different to how I thought the day would be is how utterly normal it feels in the change rooms. I've watched the last 30 AFL grand finals on television, apart from 1999 and 2006, when I was in the outer. The world outside the change rooms is bubbling and spitting like a can of Schweppes that's been shaken too hard. But in the rooms, the pre-game and half-time have felt bizarrely normal. Not flat, just normal.

After observing the relief in the players' eyes at quarter-time, the half-time break is a different vibe. Heavy breathing from fatigue partnered with a sharp focus in the eyes tells a tale of its own. Sydney got on top in that quarter with Josh Kennedy resembling the Greek god Achilles as he wrestled the game his team's way.

After a passionate address from Bevo and a few pats on the back, we send the boys back out. As the scoreboard tightens and the game finds its rhythm, I get that sickening feeling again. 'This one's going down to the wire.' I look up to the ceiling for answers or relief, I'm not entirely sure which.

I'm jolted back to the moment by the 'Chorus of Shane'. Midway into the last quarter, a chaotic piece of play unfolds on the forward flank for the Dogs. It's not pretty football – rather, a series of efforts and errors that build the tension up and up and up. At the centre of it all is Biggsy, Shane Biggs. By my count there are seven efforts from Biggsy in an inspiring minute that finishes with a Liam Picken goal. Each time Biggsy throws himself into the play, the coaches, who are a few feet away from me, call out the name 'Shane' one by one. Different voices, one name, synchronised in their spacing of each other. 'Shane!' 'SHANE!' 'Oh Shaaaane!' 'SSSHHHAAAAAANE!'

I knew we would win today. Of all the four finals, I was most confident about the big one. When the whips are cracking in the last quarter, the game is by and large played in our half. Our boys are running hard and in numbers. Our hands are fast, so damn fast. Too fast for the Swans, too fast for everyone this year.

For much of the last quarter my eyes are trained on Buddy Franklin and Dan Hannebery. I feel like these two could cause us the most damage if they get up and going. I'm inspired by how hard they're trying, both men willing their aching legs all over the field to give their club a sniff. Then the ball falls in that awkward position between Hannebery and Easton Wood. A collision, a sickening angle on Hanneberry's knee, the grimace on his face and the ball goes our way via the safe hands of our skipper. Hannebery courageously plays on, but he's hobbling and has to be taped up. It could easily have been a free kick his way for low contact, but it's a tough call. A big play from Woody.

A Jason Johannisen bomb from outside 50 is cruelly judged a point on review, and this stirs the ghosts of the past. The murmur in the crowd speaks to many of our clan believing that a curse could yet bring us down again. But not today. A colossal mark from Jordan Roughead snuffs out a momentum shift from the resulting kick-out. When Dale Morris catches Buddy by surprise with a tackle of heart and conviction, jarring the ball free, and Tom Boyd picks it up and sinks his slipper into it, I do as Denis Cometti describes in the television call. I hold my breath.

As it bounces through and the crowd goes into raptures, I sit stunned, frozen to the spot. In front of me, Chris Grant slams the desk with both palms. Three times. *Bang! Bang! Bang!* We are home. It is over. A final Liam Picken goal is the shiny, oh so shiny, cherry on top. Bevo makes the call to descend the stairs to be among our people on the bench. We make it down in record time, Rohan Smith scolding me not to do my knee again as we scamper down the internal concrete stairs.

As good as it is to watch the game from the coaches' box, the atmosphere is muffled by the walls and the glass. I noticed it up in Sydney last weekend too. Of course, you can join the dots on what's going on in the game and the buzz that reverberates through the masses, but it's not until you walk among it that you feel the warmth of the hysteria.

Emerging from the dugout behind the interchange, finding the loving arms of our club doctors Jake and Zimmer and all our support staff, brings the world into technicolour. The colours are neon red, white and blue.

14

A Stadium Holds Its Breath

On Grand Final Day, I missed the physical elements of football like a new mother misses sleep. The tangible things that form part of the soul of a footballer – dirt on the playing jumper, a corked thigh, a cut above the eyebrow. I wanted all of those things. I wanted the physical pain that goes hand in hand with the satisfaction of winning games of football.

And of course, I wanted a premiership medal.

When the siren sounded, I ran onto the MCG. It was quite a surreal experience. The 22 players who took the field that day were our heroes, and all of us, myself included, wanted to be as close to them as possible. I think I got to every player and put my arms around each one. Amid the chaos, I took a short detour over to the Swans camp to offer my condolences, but once I arrived and shook the hands of a few, I feared I'd made a mistake. When I got to Josh Kennedy, he was a broken man, tears streaming down his face. I shook his hand, apologised, and excused myself to give him space.

In the Bulldogs camp, the euphoria in the minutes after the siren was at a level I've never witnessed before and I doubt I'll ever see again. But unlike the 22 players, my emotions weren't as neatly wrapped, I suppose you could say. I felt like a witness to the scene in some ways, and I was conscious not to let any hint of self-pity float to the surface. I felt as if giving in to those personal feelings of anguish would have been disrespectful to everyone in that team, but also to everyone who wore a red, white and blue scarf that day. But there was a tightness in my smile that wasn't evident in any of my teammates' faces. They had reached a state of nirvana.

I've always said that a premiership for the Bulldogs was the biggest carrot in the game. A 62-year drought was over. We had won it. The whole club had fought and pushed and willed itself to this point. Our clan would march to the town hall. This prospect, these thoughts, had become like a mantra in my mind and gave me strength.

The whole year had felt like a moral test, and it wasn't over yet. 'Team over individual.' 'It's not about you.' 'Play your role.' Mixed emotions didn't even scratch the surface. This was an internal war, and it was raging. I repeated my mantra over and over in my head and hung on to the splinters of inner peace with a growing degree of desperation. The Dogs sat atop the football mountain as famous victors and I was a part of that, but the 22 players on the field had just become football immortals. There was a clear line between the 22 who played and the rest of us. That's just how it is in our game.

An image speaks a thousand words, or so they say. Luke Dahlhaus's reaction as the siren went will stay with me forever. Every time I see that image played, it moves me to the point of tears. Luke has such a big heart, but he can seldom find the right words to describe how he feels. He's a hugger – on and off the field. When he's really feeling it out there after kicking a goal, he'll hit his chest with a clenched fist and howl at the moon like a wolf. He means it. Dahl just tries so damn hard, he leaves it all out there on the field. He loves his club and his teammates, and when that siren sounded, he knew he was bound with both of those things forever. I wanted that too.

Hugging has become a bit of a thing at the Bulldogs these last couple of years. How do you find the perfect words in those raw moments after a game of football? Hemingway never played this game. How do you look Tom Boyd in the eye with all the madness going on around you and explain to him that his heroics in the last two hours have changed the history and future of the club you hold most dear? The simple answer is, you don't. You just put your arms around him.

In the pandemonium of victory, I bumped into my childhood hero, Tiger Matthew Richardson, who was working for Channel 7. He briefly stopped me and with great tenderness said, 'I'm feeling for you, Bob.'

Winning any grand final is dramatic. A Bulldogs premiership that breaks a 62-year drought is on another level again. How could any of us keep it together? For a lot of Bulldogs people, even daydreaming about a premiership seemed like dipping our toes in a pool of paranoid delusion. Most of us kept those dreams to ourselves. Less than two years earlier, we were the laughing stock of the league. When the reality of the result fell to the earth of our consciousness, it shook the ground beneath all of us. I know I was scrambling to stay balanced.

When Luke took over as coach at the end of 2014, the club was in crisis and the players were bruised from too many losing seasons. We'd been written off by everyone.

Early in Luke's reign, we'd flown to Coolangatta as a team for a training camp in Mooloolaba. Up to that point, Luke had been a little stand-offish with the playing group. With all the drama and carnage he'd landed in, who could blame him? It made sense to spend the first month or so just observing things, and it seemed that's exactly what he was doing.

That camp in Mooloolaba is when Luke really took control of the ship and we got a sense of the broad vision he had for all of us. At Coolangatta airport, just prior to the camp commencing, a strange thing happened. As we waited to collect our bags, one of Luke's premiership players from St Bede's in the Melbourne amateur competition spotted him and came over to say hello. Nothing strange about that, but it was the affection they showed each other that made me stop and think. It wasn't a handshake or a pat on the shoulder – they fell into a hug and held it for a few heartfelt moments. I would see this happen again with players Luke has coached. I remember thinking at the time how I wished that could be me one day.

At the core of most athletes is a need to make someone proud. Sometimes it's a parent or a sibling. Often, it's a coach. I've always described the senior coach's influence in a football club as being like that of the sun in the solar system. Everyone in the club orbits around the coach and we all draw energy from him. It's a lot on one person's shoulders, too much really, but that's how it is. Pride or affection from your coach warms you from the inside. It gets into the marrow of your bones. I wondered to myself that day in Coolangatta what it might be like to earn Luke's respect and share that sort of hug with him one day. In my experience at AFL level, a pat on the back for a job well done as you stretch out on the floor after a game was about as good as it got when it came to senior coaches sharing their affection.

A lot happened in the two years between Luke becoming coach and the Bulldogs winning the flag. We all went through a lot together. When we were down near the bottom of the ladder between 2011 and 2014, the senior players and I would often talk to the young boys coming through about how it would feel when the ship turned around and we started moving our way up the ladder. We kept encouraging them by telling them it would be the ride of their lives. But I don't think any of us imagined just how wild the ride would be.

One of the things that happened was personal, something of a spiritual connection between captain and coach. In some ways, there was no choice. With the very public breakdown in the previous relationship between Ryan Griffen and Brendan McCartney,

Luke and I had to make it work. Thankfully, we clicked almost right away. Like all of us, Luke's not perfect, but I've come to think of him as a football prophet. Spend some time with Luke and you soon realise you've never met anyone quite like him. He walks between the raindrops. I've been asked to describe him many times and I don't think I've ever come close to doing him justice. As soon as I start to speak of him, as a deeply romantic storyteller, the surfing philosopher with the eternal optimistic spirit, I hear myself and hesitate. Because, while he's all of those things, there is another side to him.

Bevo coaches with a high level of tactical sophistication and has a razor-sharp appreciation for process and protocol. I mean, he spent years working in the regulatory arm for AUSTRAC. Hardly bohemian. He pauses to find the right word. Always. He's tough. Not because he picks a fight, but because he doesn't flinch when the bell sounds. Old stories of his street-fighting past to protect young teammates float around the football world like ghost stories. In his own words, 'I've got a long fuse. Until I don't.'

How do you describe anyone in a paragraph or sound bite? My advice would be not to, but if I had to boil it down, Luke's got balance. Like all the great footballers down the line, it's their balance that gives them poise. Time to think, to wait, to make the right call. Or he could just be the love child of Eleanor Roosevelt and Gandhi, I don't know.

I don't think I ever let Luke down as a player and he never let me down as a coach. That's part of the reason why I feel closer to him than other coaches I've had, and why I like to talk and write about him. There's a purity to our partnership that was missing from the others, I guess. I let all of my other coaches down at some point. That's on me, not on them. For most of my career, I've been the sort of player who might get a bit comfortable after a few good weeks in a row. I needed regular kicks in the arse to keep me on the edge, and I duly got them. For years.

As with a lot of the best friendships in my life, Luke and I don't need to talk all that much. We just seem to agree on a lot of things that if you bundled them all up might sit under the banner of 'spirit'. In 2015 I spoke about Luke being 'the coach I always wanted to have'. It wasn't a throwaway line. I'd found a kindred spirit in my football soul.

The best example I can give is to take you into the rooms of the SCG after round five, 2015. Having won the game by a kick in torrential Sydney rain, on the road, against the odds, against a team that was always so hard to beat, we entered the rooms and celebrated with hugs and song.

This wasn't a time for pats on the back, and the coach knew it. We all held onto each other tight, we whooped and hollered. We sang our song with a guttural roar and our circle, linked by arms, jerked and swayed, such was the energy. Then we gathered in the meeting room and Bevo stood in front of us. He took a moment to compose himself, then he spoke. About simple things. He spoke about how proud he was of us. Then he started to choke back tears. He was teetering on the edge of being unable to finish his address.

It was very raw. I think so much of the Bulldogs' rise could be traced back to those tears. He had me for life after that day.

Eighteen months later, we were a premiership team. As the players went up on stage to collect their medals, I stood just off the back of the pack. The tightening in my jaw was starting to ease, the sight of our supporters crying and embracing put the enormity of what was happening in context. This was bigger than a premiership medal, bigger than a team; this was history. Maybe this was the greatest grand final story in the history of the game.

I must have known there was a chance something might happen when the moment finally arrived. I'd assumed that I might go up with the players once the cup had been presented, but it wasn't at the front of my mind. Maybe I shouldn't have been surprised about what happened next, but I was.

'I'd like to call Bob Murphy up to the stand.'

Life would never be the same again after hearing those words. The days and weeks of tension I'd held in my clenched grip suddenly let go. As hard as I'd tried to keep the pain to myself, everyone knew I was living an athlete's nightmare. In that single moment of generosity, Bevo brought me into the sunshine. The excruciating double act of hiding my obvious emotional pain and celebrating my club's greatest triumph was soothed. I didn't have to pretend anymore. Honesty sets you free, and that's what my coach did for me that day.

AFL premierships are always sprinkled with sadness. Forty-four players and 22 spots isn't a great framework for perfect harmony.

The unlucky ones who miss out feel an ache they carry with them for the rest of their days. I'm not sure that's how it should be.

As I moved towards the stage, I was swallowed up by my teammates. The noise in the stadium was thunderous and it carried me all the way up to the dais. People have asked me what that moment felt like, and it's a hard question to answer. In short, I felt everything. I felt pride – a kind of pride that's exclusive to an elder of a clan. I felt pure joy – like the joy of hearing your favourite song on the radio. I also felt aching sadness. Like the sadness that comes with the death of a friendship. All of those emotions were turned up to ten, but the difference was it was finally okay to let them out. Luke had set me free. All those things swept me away like a bit of driftwood on the Franklin River. I had no energy to go against the tide and nor did I want to. It was time to go with the flow.

Joining Easton Wood on stage opened the flood of tears. Easton is all heart. We'd leaned on each other a lot since I'd broken down earlier in the year, and I'd been like a big brother to him since he arrived at the club in 2008 as an emotional and impulsive draftee. I could not have been prouder of the way he took over the captaincy on the field after I went down. I'm sure he had bouts of self-doubt, but he played the role of skipper note-perfect, right until the final siren. At his best, Woody plays the game in a way the rest of us wish we could. Full of dare in the air and a ridiculous level of physical courage.

When I let go of Easton and turned to Luke, I bowed down to accept the medal. No words were said; we both knew the medal was arbitrary. It was all about the hug. That moment has become something of an iconic image. It stands like a mountain in my life. It's quite a thing to share such an intimate moment with someone in front of 100,000 people and millions on television. I was no longer a witness to the madness of this historic premiership triumph; I was right in the middle of the damn thing.

I've come to think of the medal Luke placed around my neck as the medal for the 23rd man. I wasn't the only Bulldog player to miss out on something that day. What gives me a sense of peace now is thinking of that moment and that medal as a symbol for all the efforts of not just every player on our list in 2016, but every player who has ever pulled on the Western Bulldogs/Footscray jumper and missed out on a premiership. It's for Mitch Wallis, Jack Redpath and Josh Prudden, but it's also for Simon Garlick, Scott Wynd and Merv Hobbs.

Luke has said he simply wanted me to feel a part of the premiership. Maybe the gesture describes the essence of Luke's heart in a way that words can't. For a brief moment, in a stadium filled with 100,000 people watching the most competitive sport in the country, there was an unmistakable communal feeling of love. Everything was in perfect harmony, and that is a rare diamond in professional sport.

Fittingly, our club legend and this Bulldogs team's hero, John Schultz, handed the cup to Easton and me, and we lifted it up to the heavens. The sons and daughters of Footscray released 62 years of pain and frustration into the sky with a euphoric roar. Every single one of us howled at the moon. We all meant it.

It was time to wreck our dancing shoes. The party had just begun and it lit up like fireworks. Any sadness I felt was put in a box – it was time to get a drink and dance like no-one was watching. Everyone on the field took off for the lap of honour and you could feel the love in the outer. It was a beautiful kind of hysteria. I wanted total fucking anarchy at this point. Forget about the security guards, people, get yourselves out on the ground and do the two-step with me! Be here now! It was that kind of vibe.

I got about halfway around the MCG when I remembered I had my playing jumper on underneath my snazzy zip-up jacket. I'd put the jumper on in the first place to indulge in the pain. Now it was time to revel in the thrill of it all.

I showed my colours. And our supporters lapped it up. I think they understood what it meant too. We were all one and the same, we were a clan united in a victory dance. All the pain and heartache from the past was evaporating into the air. The weight of history, the burden, was lifted from our shoulders. The war had been won. Bulldogs people held onto each other, desperate to share the moment. Savour it. There were no strangers in the MCG after the siren sounded. If you had the tricolours on, we were brothers and sisters. Sons and daughters of the mighty West.

Thursday, 23 March 2017: Northcote

There are lots of eyes on me this year. God, I'm nervous.

Can I still play? That's the question. I'm 34 years old, soon to be 35, and I'm making a comeback from a second knee reconstruction. Why did I let people talk me into going around again?

I retired three times last year. Each time I let the decision sit there for a few days, spoke to lots of different people, and they all said I should go on. The bastards. Eventually the tug of optimism dragged me back. 'Imagine if I could help us go back to back ...' It's a big carrot to have dangling in front of you.

Why do athletes have such a hard time letting go? It might have something to do with the fact that retiring feels a lot like quitting, and we're built, physically and emotionally, never to give up. But doesn't there come a point when you're not quitting, but simply moving on to something else? So why is it so hard? Maybe it's because a lifetime of dedication to the skills and nuances of the game will become worthless the moment you stop. The ball skills, body positioning and physical endurance you've trained since you were a little tacker go in the bin. That seems like such a waste.

Maybe it's something a bit more unsavoury – maybe it's ego. The thought of turning the bright lights of the stage off is just too much to bear. A life in the shadows is a life forgotten, is it not? It's a perverse thought and not entirely accurate, but that's a side effect of how athletes are built too. We love the attention, crave it even.

Sadly, it's probably all of those things that have dragged me back to this brutal game. I'm still captain, and of course, there's the aching hole in my stomach of unfinished business. I missed out on the premiership last year, in case you didn't know. Yeah, I'm that guy. So, as I sit here in my lounge room looking down the barrel of another long season in which anything can and will happen, I feel like only a premiership will do. That is the only way I can 'win' this year.

The TV flickers in front of me. The Tigers are playing the Blues. I look at the players smashing into each other and think, 'I don't know if I can do that anymore.' These past few months, I've navigated my knee rehabilitation and the longest pre-season in AFL history and I've felt pretty good, but until you perform when it matters you can't really be sure you're still up to it. I'm scared. Afraid I'll embarrass myself and let people down.

Ever since I learnt to ride my bike at the age of three, I've always trusted my physicality. The athleticism to run, jump and evade. But playing AFL football at 34 feels like trying to outrun the sunset. The lights are going out; it's just a matter of when. For every Dustin Fletcher or Brent Harvey who played into their late 30s, there are countless others who fell off the cliff, and I've watched it happen to so many. One minute they look okay; the next they're gone. The heart is willing, but the legs just don't have it in them. I watched the game swallow up one of my predecessors, Brad Johnson, like a king tide sweeps away a sandcastle.

What do they say about veterans when the end is nigh? 'He's lost a yard.' But if it was just losing a yard or two, I wouldn't be fearful about the year ahead, but that's not the whole story. Mistakes or shortcomings on the football field are always directly related to confronting emotions. If, for instance, you lose your speed or endurance, that might mean you can't chase hard enough when you need to. You'll look lazy or selfish. If your reflexes start to dim you might flinch at the critical moment and announce to the football world that you're a coward.

I don't know if I've lost a yard. I don't know if I'll flinch at the critical moment against the Magpies tomorrow night. But I'm scared that the lights could go out at any moment. I don't want to look like a coward.

I'm already the guy who missed out on the premiership. How will it look if I also lose the hunger to compete at this level?

All that said, I'm almost entirely certain this AFL season will be my last. And recent newspaper reports about a more hardline approach from the World Anti-Doping Association are a sign it's time for me to wind up my playing career, if ever there was one. They want to ban caffeine!

I am what would be generally considered a clean athlete. I play by the rules. I'm old enough to remember watching Canadian sprinter Ben Johnson crouched down at the starters' blocks in the 100-metre final of the 1988 Seoul Olympic Games. I remember the pure exhilaration of watching as a six-year-old as he powered away from the fastest men on the planet. I also remember the shame and disappointment that engulfed sport and sports lovers in the aftermath of Johnson's positive drug test.

I want a clean game. But if you want to ban my morning coffee because of its performance-enhancing attributes, then I'll have to bow out. My old teammate Ben Harrison used to say, 'If that's wrong, I don't wanna be right.' I defer to Harro.

There have been controls around caffeine for my whole playing career. Because of its obvious stimulant powers, there is a limit to how much you can ingest before a game. It only takes a few bad apples to ruin it for everyone, and I'm sure there are more than a few athletes around the globe abusing caffeine via powders or tablets. But that's a long way away from my morning coffee order: strong flat white with full-cream milk.

I read Paul Kelly's memoir *How to Make Gravy* a few years back and was intrigued by part of his routine when on tour. As a travelling troubadour, Kelly spends many months a year on the road, and part of his ritual is that whenever he finds himself in a new city or town he walks to the river or waterway as an anchor point for his body and mind.

It wasn't until I read Kelly's book that I realised I'd been doing the same thing as a travelling half-back flanker for years, except it isn't dirty brown water I go looking for but a decent cup of coffee. Serves the same purpose: it puts your feet on the pavement and gets some fresh air in your lungs. Whether it's a cold river or a hot cup, sometimes you just need to tie your rope to something sturdy and familiar.

Playing for the Bulldogs has had its ups and downs – we've had to beg, borrow and probably metaphorically steal a bit just to keep afloat in the AFL. Part of that desperation has seen us play games far and wide – farther and wider than most clubs, it would be fair to say. I've seen a lot of Australia as a footballer. We've sold games in Darwin, Cairns and Canberra. And I've sought out a brew in each of those places.

I've walked the streets of Adelaide on a Saturday morning in search of coffee, and after 30 minutes of despair become convinced I'd settle for any signs of life in that sleepy town. I've walked the romantic, foggy and steep streets of Launceston looking for that magical cup to give me the strength to face the might of the Hawthorn footy club. And I found the best cup of coffee I've ever had in a dirty, shitty arcade in Cairns.

Coffee, like life and chocolates, throws up a few surprises. Many times, the desperate search for my drug of choice has been a solo journey, the solitude singing in harmony with the 'stuff', but often it's a bonding experience to be shared with others. Boredom was my gateway to the caffeine underworld.

As an 18-year-old aspiring footballer, I buddied up with one of my young Bulldogs comrades, Patrick Bowden, and we had a rare talent for wasting time. Between training sessions, we'd go in search of Melbourne's thriving café culture and set up camp somewhere. At first, I didn't even like the taste of it – coffee was what my parents and their friends drank. But Pat was very gentle with me, and with the help of teaspoons and sugar he filled my cup and I was swept away by its smooth, velvety buzz.

Before long, I went from an occasional cappuccino with Pat to a daily morning hit among strangers. Over time, I dispensed with the sugar – I needed it straight. The hand of caffeine took a firm grip on me. I was swallowed up by its beauty and offered little resistance to its charms. Over the years, I've purchased various coffee machines – percolators, pods and the like – but I still love the ritual of seeking a professional to hook me up. Most of the enjoyment I draw from my cuppa is the anticipation. A ten-minute stroll through wind and rain is terribly romantic when you're chasin'.

I've bonded with my baristas over the years, too. When I moved to North Fitzroy in the early 2000s, I struck up a partnership with Martha, who ran 'the corner store'. Martha opened early (6 am), and this was at a time when Justine had moved in with me and we didn't have kids. We used to wake up early and go for a walk through the streets surrounding Edinburgh Gardens before settling in at the corner store for coffee and advice from Martha. The regulars there were like a dawn take on Billy Joel's 'Piano Man'. Everyone had a story.

Just down the road from Martha's is the Tin Pot Café, and the barista around this time was a rockabilly blues man known as Mick. Mick's coffee was as slick as his quiff, but he also introduced me to lots of great music. I'd sit in the front bay window, eat breakfast and drink coffee with the world passing by to the sounds of Tex Perkins' first solo album. There, multiple love affairs began smashing into each other in a cosmic storm.

At the turn of the decade, we crossed Nicholson Street into the more conservative world of Carlton North, although our hearts remained on the east side of the divide. Our coffee dealers became a couple of charismatic Lebanese characters, Johnny and Bhudi. By this time Justine and I were in baby mode and coffee became less a recreation and more like the first cousin of oxygen. We didn't just want it; we needed it. Johnny and Bhudi opened even earlier than Martha, and I leaned on them a lot as I walked the pram with one of our babies rugged up in the front while Justine got some sleepy respite at home.

At the footy club, a cup of coffee is often used as an olive branch – what tea and sympathy used to be for baby boomers, I suppose. With injuries, selection, personality clashes and the general pressure of a life in the spotlight, this game takes its toll on the emotional reserves of us all. So many times, 'Let's grab a coffee' has been the impetus for a positive turn in the fortunes of a young player or an ageing veteran. Like all addictions, though, there is a dark side to its allure. I had my brush with the devil.

I got a wriggle on with my coffee intake from those innocent days with Pat Bowden. I quickly became a two-cups-a-day guy. I never missed, and still to this day one of the first thoughts when I open my eyes of a morning is, 'Mmm, coffee ...'

When my knee troubles started in 2006, some of the game's innocence – and of life itself, if I'm honest – was lost a little. By the time the 2009 season rolled around, one of my knees was in such bad shape I had to have it injected with local anaesthetic every week just to play. I hated football at this time, and the idea of getting myself up to play each week filled me with a thudding dread.

Week after week, I knew that in a few days' time I'd have to slide up onto the doctor's bench on game day and clench my fists as the needle slid into my patella tendon. Sometimes things went smoothly – the needle went in with little fuss and I was able to run, jump and kick with the freedom I'd enjoyed for years. But there were many other days and nights when things went awry. The needle would often hit something in my knee and shards of pain would light the joint up. I'd play mistake-riddled games with a limp and a head full of dark clouds.

During those years I began to use coffee as a marker of time. Like I said, I was a 'two coffees a day' man, so if I was playing on a Saturday and it was Wednesday, I kept a little bean counter in my mind that I had eight coffees to come until they stuck the needle in again. Those coffees were like tiny little dotted islands in a sea of anguish. Sands of relief. Looking back, I suppose I was depressed, or at least extremely anxious. Eventually my knee began to heal and I didn't need injections to play, but those times left a few scars.

Entering my 18th year of this football odyssey, I'm happy to say I don't use coffee as a marker of dreaded time anymore, and the kids are grown up enough now that we walk to the coffee shop at a reasonable hour. I'm breaking in a new barista too, a Kiwi guy who makes a great cup on top of the hill in Northcote, our new home.

So I think I'll get out just in time before WADA brings down the heavy hand of the law. Which is just as well, because we've got a few road trips ahead of us again this year, and I'll need to go searching one last time for my morning fix.

This game leaves us all, but I don't like the chances of me giving up my precious vice. And I'm proud to say that my idea of paradise is the same as the great 'Man in Black', Johnny Cash, who when asked, 'What is paradise?' answered, 'This morning, with her, having coffee.' Amen.

15

You Don't Get to Choose Your Own Nickname

There's an unwritten rule within footy clubs and it is this: you don't get to pick your own nickname. I know, because I've tried to do it myself.

In 2010, when bustling Barry Hall joined the Bulldogs, the two of us hatched a plan. The idea was for Barry to start a rumour that I, the skinny flanker, was a formidable boxer, a renowned pugilist. Barry has always had some credentials in this area; only months earlier, playing for the Sydney Swans, he had dramatically knocked out Brent Staker of the West Coast Eagles. That, and the fact it was assumed Barry would go on to a serious boxing career when his playing days were done, made him the perfect candidate to vouch for my talent inside the ring.

A rumour is one thing, but we needed a hook to get people on board. So we came up with the idea of a nickname. I offered up a suggestion: 'Butch'. Barry just smiled his knowing smile that makes people feel safe and scared at the same time. And I became Butch. I was really hoping the nickname would take off, but alas it never did. I see Barry around every so often and he always calls me Butch which makes us both smile, but I don't think anyone else has ever called me by that name. The rumour of my boxing prowess went down in the first round too. It's disappointing, but that's the rule – you don't get to pick your own nickname.

The language inside a football club's change rooms keeps to a different rhythm than the chatter outside its walls. If a footy team was a racing car, the banter inside the locker room would be like the lubricating motor oil. It helps keep things moving smoothly.

In April 2017 I did a weekly spot on SEN radio with Garry Lyon, Hamish McLachlan and Tim Watson. My task was to come up with a top five every Wednesday morning. In my second week, I listed my top five favourite footy club nicknames, after some of the most enjoyable research I've done in my life. I spoke to a whole lot of different people beforehand about some of the blokes they'd played with and their accompanying nicknames. Here is the final five:

5: 'Lacka', as in 'lacka brains'.

4: 'Harvey Norman', because apparently there was a young bloke out Gisborne way who showed 'no interest'.

3: 'The Mailman', given to a bloke who was well built, had a booming kick and trained well, but just couldn't get a kick when it came to the real stuff. He was the Mailman because he 'didn't deliver on weekends'.

2: 'The Lantern', because he was 'not too bright and had to be carried'. It's believed The Lantern may also be Harvey Norman. (This remains unconfirmed.)

1: 'Clock'. This gets the gold medal, a nickname given to a bloke who had one arm longer than the other. I love Clock. It's perfect. There's true beauty in its simplicity.

When the list was delivered on air, listeners were asked to send in some of their own favourites and a couple stood out. An overweight country footballer who wore number 11 on his back was affectionately called 'Brackets'. And another bloke was called 'Blisters', because he showed up after the hard work was done.

We've had some good ones over the years at the Bulldogs. Veteran Matty Boyd is known simply as 'Keith'; the only real story to it is that it's his middle name. Ben Harrison made the discovery and word quickly spread during a Whitten Oval skills session. The hysteria reached its climax with players struggling to execute simple kicking drills. There was just something about the sound of the name 'Keith' that offset Matty's then serious vibe. Again, it was all in the simplicity. That was in 2003 and I'm proud to say he's been Keith ever since.

Probably the most practical use for a good nickname is how it helps a young draftee connect with the group. It's a great honour to have a brand-new nickname bestowed upon you when you join a footy club. The Bulldogs, like most footy clubs, have a proud history of this. In 2015 we had a bumper crop. As has now become tradition, when the new draftees came into the club on their first day, Bevo introduced them to all of us and then asked the young lads if they had any nicknames yet. This fresh litter of pups got off to a slow start.

Our first pick that year was Josh Dunkley, the son of Sydney Swans gun Andrew Dunkley. When Josh was asked for his nickname, he limply replied 'Dunks'. 'Hmm, that won't do at all,' I thought. Our next pick was a big, strong boy from the Dandenong Stingrays, Kieren Collins. When he was asked for his nickname, all he could offer up was 'Collo'. There were audible murmurs of discontent within the playing ranks.

True leadership is sensing the moment to act, and it happened that I was sitting next to our next pick in the draft, Bailey Williams. Bailey was a promising young, athletic defender from Glenelg. I leaned across and whispered in his ear that he should tell Bevo his nickname was 'Horse'. I suspected Bailey was going to offer up 'Willo' or 'Bails', and that simply wouldn't fly. The mob were thirsty for blood and I was sure that 'Willo' would fall flat and that 'Horse' would rip the roof off.

When Bailey's moment came, he shouted out 'HORSE' from the back of the room almost before Bevo had finished asking him the question. All the boys let out an appreciative roar, just as I'd envisioned. It was a glorious moment. Although to this day I'm still not sure if I helped Horse or bullied him.

A few weeks later, at the official Western Bulldogs season launch at Crown Casino, I sat at a table with the top brass – club president Peter Gordon and his wife, Kerri, and AFL CEO Gillon McLachlan and his wife, Laura. We ate, drank, and watched on, clapping as each player was brought on stage to receive their jumper for the upcoming season. Towards the end of the formalities, the number 34 was called out and Bailey Williams confidently strode onto the stage to take his jumper from club great Scott West and Bevo. Having your photo taken with your very first Bulldogs jumper is a special moment for any player.

After the photo, MC Luke Darcy motioned Bailey over towards him for a short interview. At this point I wasn't concerned at all about what was about to happen. That was until Luke asked the question: 'Have the boys given you a nickname yet?' I panicked. I could feel my face turning red and I could see that Bailey was flushed too.

There was an awkward moment of silence before Bailey started his answer. 'Oh geez, yeah, um, this feels like a bit of a stitch-up ... Um, well, actually our captain Bob Murphy gave me a nickname – it's "Horse".'

Silence.

A few things happened at that moment. The first thing I noticed were gasps in the audience, due to Horse being a pretty crude moniker given out in footy clubs, relating to the size of a man's penis. This didn't please some people in the audience, oh no, it did not. Darce quickly wrapped up the interview, sensing it had gone sour. I felt my own core temperature rise sharply, and I was on the worst possible table in the packed Palladium room for this to happen (although I do recall Peter Gordon finding the whole thing very humorous, which eased some anxiety for me).

I was told later by Lachie Hunter that a woman on his table had scoffed at the nickname, before hissing, 'That's disgusting!'

At the time, I was deeply worried that Bailey's mum or dad might be in the room. Mercifully, they were both back home in Glenelg. The fact I was the captain made it a lot more inappropriate and, it has to be said, a lot funnier, but the laughs were never going to translate beyond the walls of the club. Still, if Bailey goes on to play 100 games for the Bulldogs, which I think he will, there's a very good chance that the number 34 locker will read Bailey 'Horse' Williams. In my humble, immature opinion, that's a great legacy. For both of us.

It's also worth noting that by the end of their very first week at the club, 'Dunks' was 'Ken' due to his resemblance to Barbie's offsider, and 'Collo' was 'Dad', because it was hard to believe he was genuinely 17: to our eyes, he looked older than the veterans.

You can get a nickname a hundred different ways, and creating them is a sport in itself. There's an enormous amount of pride if you can get a nickname to stick, but at the same time it can be just as enjoyable to give a player a nickname that only you call him by. It's a little connection and sometimes the little things are the best.

How Lindsay Gilbee could end up with the nickname 'Loose Toast' still staggers me. Shortened to 'Toast' these days, it stemmed from Lindsay's habit at breakfast of waiting until everyone had feasted on the piping hot toast after Monday recovery at the Melbourne Sports and Aquatic Centre in Albert Park. When the crowd thinned, Lindsay would drift up and pick up what was left over. This caught the attention of Paul Hudson, who called it a 'loose toast get'. Uncontested toast. It stuck.

On a pre-season camp in Ballarat, we were given a talk one night on professionalism and the importance of a healthy diet. At the breakfast buffet the next morning, we all lined up for something to eat, but the tray of bacon was wisely avoided by almost everyone. One of my '99 draft alumni, Patrick Wiggins, swiped a piece of bacon from the tray and rolled it into a ball. With a quick look around the room to see if he was being watched, he then shovelled it into his mouth. Unfortunately for big Pat, someone was watching. Someone is always watching in a footy club. And so Pat earned himself the nickname 'Kevin'.

One of my all-time favourite nicknames belongs to Lin Jong. Lin, Dale Morris and myself travelled to country Victoria on a pre-season community camp and visited an aged care facility. The knockabout bumpkin who was our tour guide introduced himself and stuck out his hand to greet us. We introduced ourselves as Dale, Bob and Lin. Our tour guide paused a moment and said, 'It's a pleasure to meet you, Dale, Bob, and ... Glen.' I had to turn away to hide my glee. Lin has been Glen ever since, Glenys on special occasions.

On the very same day as 'Glen-gate', we made one final promotional stop in Melton before heading home. This was a handball competition at the local post office. We climbed out of the car, tired from a couple of long days preaching the gospel of the Bulldogs, and were confronted by a big sign out the front of the post office that lifted our spirits to the heavens. 'Handball competition from 3–4 pm with Western Bulldogs players Dale Morris, Robert Murphy and Lin *Gong*.'

Glen knows how much I enjoy people mispronouncing his name, and occasionally I'll get a text from Glen that contains a picture of a bill or invoice he has received with different variations of his name. He tells me that his local Thai restaurant has had such a hard time getting it right, he just goes with whatever version they've come up with.

'Pad Thai for Tim?'

'Yep, that'll do.'

Gets me every time.

There are almost as many ways to get a nickname in a footy club as there are actual nicknames. Most of the time they're derived from the 'Big Two' – either a physical trait (think Sticks, Pigeon or Barrel), or a play on words from someone's actual name. Joel Corey from the Cats goes by 'Smithy', because his Geelong teammates thought he had no last name.

They are the Big Two, but there are many other mutations of the art form. My personal favourite is the rolling nickname, where a name morphs over time into various other form. Sometimes a 'roller' can continue to morph months and even years later, and very occasionally there's what I call a 'hot roller'. It happened to Nathan Brown during a training session at the Kennel. When we ran out to train his nickname was the highly sophisticated 'Browny', but by the time we were stretching down on the fence he was 'Chicken Parma'.

Simon Garlick did most of the heavy lifting that day, while Gia and I chipped in with a few suggestions and the background laughter. 'Garlo' started referring to Browny as 'Nath' just to annoy him, but it quickly escalated from there. Between the kicking and handball drills we got on a hot roller. Nath turned into Nate and it took off like a bushfire: Nate, NATO, Napalm, Palmer, Arnold Palmer, Chicken Parma. That was a rare day, a good day.

One of the unluckier blokes on the nickname front was Scotty Welsh. Traded to the Bulldogs from the Crows, we used to wind him up a bit about the city of Adelaide and we discovered that he had a deep love of Devon sandwiches, otherwise known as 'fritz and sauce'. I'd never really heard that phrase before, so 'Fritz' seemed like a good leaping-off point for a nickname. For a few months, Scott was Fritz and all was well in the world. Then the world was horrified by the grisly discovery of paedophile monster Josef Fritzel and his house of hidden horrors in Austria. All of a sudden, the calls of 'Fritzel!' in the locker room and out on the field lost their innocent charm.

'Our' Fritz was a little bit anxious about the whole thing and one day pleaded with Huddo and I to have the nickname overturned. We heard him out, and just as he'd finished his monologue Rocket Eade walked past, patted him on the back and said, 'Hey, *Fritzel*!' Fritz hung his head, dejected.

One of the anxieties associated with joining a club is picking up the tempo and language of the locker room. Everyone is trying to find their place in this little world. I always used nicknames as a way of easing new players into the club. The name itself was almost arbitrary; it was a subtle way to connect.

Saturday, 25 March 2017: Northcote

I've done it – survived my first 'proper' game in almost a year, a scratchy but solid win over the plucky Magpies last night. And now it feels good to wind down on the couch after a quiet day at home with Justine and the kids, nursing the sweet soreness that comes from playing a game of footy. I'm as happy as a pup with two tails as we sprawl out on the couch, nursing a couple of glasses of pinot, while the Demons are running away with it against the Saints at Etihad Stadium.

The warmth of the setting and the wine quickly evaporate when I see Saint Nick Riewoldt's knee buckle under him. It sends a cold shiver through me, seeing him clutch his leg. The dread that washes over him looks eerily familiar to my own situation almost 12 months ago to the day. There's an unmistakable sense of resignation on Nick's face as the buggy removes him from the field. I wonder whether he contemplates waving goodbye. Of all the people watching from their couches, I feel like I might be the only one who knows exactly what's going on inside his head.

I've known Nick for a long time. We started in the AFL at about the same time, have some mutual friends and bump into each other on occasion. We became close after the 2015 International Rules tour, when we spent a week in New York and a week in Dublin. The tour was one of the most enjoyable fortnights I've had, made even more special because the players' partners were an integral part of the touring party. There was a great sense of camaraderie on and off the field, and some of the friendships made on that trip have endured.

Nick's wife, Cath, is a 188-cm Texan with a warm spirit and an enchanting southern drawl. Smart as a whip, Cath has made me laugh a lot in the short time I've known her, and not just because of her occasional blind spots or slight misfires with Aussie slang. (It's taking 'the' piss, Cath, not taking 'a' piss.)

Seeing Nick injured like this is no laughing matter. Justine and I are rooted to the couch feeling sick for our friends. It looks like it might be the end. I send Cath a message to say that we're thinking of them and that we are here to help if they need anything. As is always the way, the game waits for no-one, and as the Demons celebrate their win and the Hawks and Bombers start up for their Saturday night round one clash, we wait for bits of information to drip through.

Suddenly the noises from the Saints' rooms start sounding optimistic. Before long, Saint Nick is being interviewed by Fox Footy's David King and talking in terms of having 'dodged a bullet'. The Saints seem confident he's ruptured his capsule but sustained no damage to the ACL. I can feel a collective sigh of relief go through the entire football universe.

Twenty minutes later, my phone rings and it's Nick. The relief in his voice is tangible. He speaks about the waves of consequences that washed over him as he rolled off the stadium. No more game, no more season, no more football, no premiership. It's a lot for anyone to process, let alone someone as intensely driven for football silverware and personal satisfaction as Nick. He really has dodged a bullet; the light that burns in all athletes is still flickering. He'll be sore tomorrow, but at least there is a tomorrow.

16

We Are Family

I was born with crooked little fingers. At the top knuckle of both hands, the pinky takes a sharp turn in towards the ring finger. Our three children, Jarvis, Frankie and Delilah, have crooked little fingers too. I love those little physical signatures handed down the genetic line. Mercifully, our children look more like their mother, Justine, than me, but along with their little fingers they've got my eyes.

I had a heavy crush on Justine Quigley from the first time I met her at that school disco in 1994, but we weren't a couple until much later. Perhaps because we'd both secretly assumed that we would one day end up together, we got serious quickly when we reconnected. Within a year, Justine had moved in with me in North Fitzroy, we'd travelled through Europe and we were pregnant. Two weeks before Justine told me the big news, we had a conversation about kids. 'Let's wait ten years.' A fortnight later: 'Change of plans!'

As any first-time parent will tell you, that first pregnancy is a bit daunting, but we were so happy. We had known we would have kids eventually, we were in love and in this thing for the long haul, so we were very excited.

In the lead-up to the birth, we wrote lists of names for both boys and girls. On the advice of my brother-in-law, Souma, we didn't find out the sex ahead of time. 'Seeing your child for the first time is the greatest feeling in the world, and *then* you find out if it's a boy or a girl and it takes that euphoria even higher,' Souma told us. He was right.

On our list of names was one of my suggestions: Jarvis. I liked the sound the letters made, I adored their shape when you wrote them down, and of course Jarvis Cocker (from Pulp) is one of the coolest cats on this earth. And he's a skinny bloke too. Justine wasn't going for it at all, but I wore her down by talking to her belly using the name – as a joke, really.

The moment we saw Jarvis was just as Souma had described, but the labour took two and a half days. I described it at the time as 'a festival of pain and anguish'. Jarvis was posterior (the back of his head was facing Justine's back), so the birth was a difficult one and the pain in Justine's back was excruciating. My job for much of the festival was to keep heat packs on her lower back. For hours. After a while I could feel my own back seizing up. I was acutely aware that any ailment I had wasn't relevant, but I couldn't escape a sense of dread: 'My back is giving out!' Between contractions, I had a quick stretch to relieve the pain. My pain!

Justine's head shot around. 'Are you okay?'

'I'm great. You're doing an amazing job!'

Meeting our baby boy washed the pain away (although I don't know if Justine would say the same). It's quite a thing to witness a birth. To see the love of your life go through that much agony is as difficult as it is inspiring. My wife is one tough cookie. A heroine.

Jarvis Benjamin Murphy was born at 5 am, and while Justine dozed I held him in my arms overlooking the hills of Heidelberg as the sun came up on the horizon. It was a perfect morning. In the days that followed, I was shocked to see in the newspapers that life outside our hospital room was continuing as normal. I was incensed. Our baby boy was a man-on-the-moon moment!

A year after Jarvis was born, on a trip to Byron Bay, I proposed to Justine on the beach trail near Suffolk Park. Just as I was about to take a knee, someone ran past us exclaiming, 'A whale is breaching!' Justine took off towards the drama in the water, but I was committed to the proposal. I grabbed her hand, startled her, hurriedly declared my love and asked her to marry me. She said yes, but we missed seeing the whale. Marriage is about sacrifice and compromise.

A few months later, we got married at T'Gallant winery in Red Hill on the Mornington Peninsula. Instead of a wedding speech, I changed the lyrics to Paul Kelly's 'When I First Met Your Ma' to fit our story. My teammate Dylan Addison played guitar and I did my best on vocals. It was a song for Jarvis and my stunning bride.

Befitting his name, our Jarvis is a true original. He's ten now, a gentle soul, sensitive and creative. I admire Jarvis for lots of reasons, but the thing that sticks out is that he has passion for his interests and doesn't just follow the crowd. There's plenty of iceberg under the tip. He barracks for the Bulldogs (it's kind of a rule in our house), but he doesn't share the football bug. Lego, cartoon drawings, bird watching, lizard appreciation, reading and tree climbing head his list of interests right now, and I can't wait to see how those evolve over time.

When Jarvis goes to stay at his nan's house in Tynong, he likes to sit up in one tree in particular and read his books. It's the exact same spot where his mum read her books as a child. He went up that tree instinctively, into that exact spot, without knowing the family significance. Just like crooked little fingers: that stuff makes my heart smile.

Jarvis is a country boy at heart. For a few years we lived in a cramped townhouse in Carlton North. On returning from a trip out of town, Jarvis told me, 'Dad, in the country your backyard is the whole world. But in the city it's just a fence.' We moved to a bigger place very soon after.

If any football club culture has seeped into our house it's probably most obvious in nicknames. Jarvis was J-Bone for years, until one day he announced that he didn't like it. I didn't have the heart to tell him you don't get to choose your own nickname, but on a recent beach holiday we went out for lunch and J-Bone regularly ordered chicken nuggets. On the 12th occassion, Justine swooped in. 'Maybe we should just call you "Nugget".' And so he's Nugget – for now, anyway.

Jarvis was born on 15 October 2007. Two years later, on 21 November, Frances Jean Murphy joined the clan. Her birth was fast, smooth and orthodox. Her life has been anything but. Her older brother was a calm baby who ate well and slept through the night. We tried to get Frances, or Frankie, on the same routine, but she wouldn't have any of it. I'm sure if she'd had the words, she would have told her tired and frustrated parents, 'There's a new sheriff in town!'

Right from the start, we dubbed Frankie 'Fire and Ice'. She can be the most loving, affectionate soul you could ever meet. Then with the swish of her ponytail and a 'look' she'll slice you in half. For a brief period as a toddler, Frankie was nicknamed 'The Wrecker' as a way of soothing her brother's pain after he'd built his wooden blocks to epic proportions, only for The Wrecker to breeze in and destroy the construction. In recent years, she's taken on the more artistic rhythm of 'Frankie Lanky Lou' or 'Schnooka'.

Frank is our resident thespian, gymnast and entertainer. She likes to sing and do cartwheels. She's already an accomplished ballet dancer, and a future on a stage somewhere could well be on the cards. I could listen to Frankie sing all day long, which is just as well, because she does. The 'Fire and Ice' is still evident and we wouldn't have it any other way.

I recently took Frankie's training wheels off her bike and within ten minutes she was riding without my help. I felt quite emotional as she nervously pedalled away from me. Those little moments force you to reflect, and they also help shade in the portrait of your parents and how they brought you up. Having said that, this day and that first bike ride were all about Frankie. Her smile said it all.

'The world just got bigger, Dad. What else is out there?' Soon after, she was off riding through the park with ease. 'Atta girl,' I thought.

Frankie has a knack for stuff; she's a natural. But of course the inevitable crash came a few minutes later, and it was a good tumble too, complete with bike on top of twisted body, and legs entwined in the steel of the frame and the serrated edge of the chain. I jogged over and asked if she was hurt and needed a rest. 'No, Dad, gotta get back on the bike, it's the Murphy way!' I was still audibly laughing as she rode off with grazes on her palms, a few scrapes on her knees and her little legs pumping. I don't recall those specific words ever being said in our house. My best guess is that getting back on the bike is Frankie's way of paraphrasing what she's seen in her short life at home. But it might have just been the excitement of the day.

In the hospital after Justine had given birth to our third child, Delilah, I noticed in the nurses' notes that the birth was described as 'natural'. I'm not so sure. To my eyes, it looked like a four-hour bull ride. It was quick, painful and wild. In the hospital, I played my daughter 'Handle With Care' by the Traveling Wilburys. I wanted little Delilah's first song to be one of gentle optimism.

For the first 18 months of her time on earth, Justine and I convinced ourselves that our youngest would be the 'peaceful and calm' one. Eventually we conceded defeat and Delilah was branded 'The Hurricane', which has evolved to 'Boombaloom'. Just as a lava lamp constantly moves, Delilah doesn't sit still. Ever. Every night, even now, Delilah will wake up and wander into our room for cuddles.

We feign annoyance, but secretly crave her presence. She's taken this role in the family from Frankie. To steal a line from Jerry Seinfeld, sleeping next to Delilah is a bit like sleeping next to a goat in a laundry bag. Legs, feet, elbows and fists can shoot off in any direction.

She's not quite four years old, but already we can tell she's smart as a whip. Keen to make up the ground on her older brother and sister. An hour with Delilah is the full parenting experience, but if she wants to charm you, you've got no hope. She charms us a lot. On my little walks up to Delilah's kindergarten, she picks two purple flowers from the same spot every time. One for me, one for her. I've started putting them in a safe place for fear that one day she'll stop giving them to me. Sentimental fool.

Raising kids is hard. Unrelenting. But those little moments you share with your children, when you really connect, are like purple flowers in your heart. There are times when the kids are all playing together on the trampoline and Justine and I are nursing a glass of wine on the back veranda, when we'll shoot each other a smile, not unlike Frankie's, that says it all. 'Look what we did! How lucky are we?' The balance is always quickly restored by an unwanted double bounce or a poke in the eye, but that's the way it's gotta be.

I think Justine and I would be happy enough if our kids were healthy, kind to people and followed their passions in life. We're lucky, because they're already so much more.

*

In 2015, 13 years after representing Australia in Ireland and discovering the Irish in me, I was there again with our country's crest on my chest. It was a different experience this time around, maybe because I was much older, a father and a husband. The players' partners travelled with them this time, and we spent a week in New York preparing and bonding, before touching down in Dublin. I was intrigued by how it would feel to be back in the motherland. I hesitate to use such cheesy language, but almost immediately it felt like home. I don't feel like that when I travel anywhere else. I trust that instinct.

The 2015 tour was incredible. The touring party bonded instantly, and having the women there made it even more special. There were nights out, of course, but it wasn't as hedonistic as it had been 13 years ago. I think seeing Justine make beautiful friendships with so many of the women on that trip made it extra special. She's kept in touch with quite a few of them, and a lot of the friendships from that tour have endured for me too. Luke Hodge, Eddie Betts, Nick Smith and Joey Montagna are three guys I'd never really spent much time with before but now call them friends. But it was Nick Riewoldt and Jarryd Roughead who I bonded with most. I now consider them two of my closest friends. A two-week International Rules football tour is a bit like a honeymoon for friendship. It's all of the best things about football condensed into two weeks, so there's not enough time to get sick of each other or wear each other down. All of your old jokes are new again and the laughs flow easily.

Nick and I laugh at ourselves that we are the two sad guys of the AFL, forever linked with not winning a premiership. The misery twins. We're quite different in lots of ways, but that can be a great thing in a friendship. He laughs and makes people laugh a lot more than you might think. I was asked to describe Nick recently, and without a thought said, 'Half man, half horse, all heart.' For a very serious, driven person, Nick is very warm and affectionate. Roughy, I knew I would be mates with before I got to know him. Sometimes you can just tell. That might be an Irish thing as well. He's easy company and he makes people feel good about themselves. He's had about as much success in footy as anyone ever has, but he carries no arrogance around with him. He has endured a lot over the last couple of years, but mercifully he's made it through to the other side. It was difficult, but also a privilege to be his friend while he and his beautiful wife, Sarah, navigated that traumatic period.

As a Quigley, Justine is Irish too, although, like me, she hadn't paid much heed to it growing up. I think she was also shocked by how Irish she looked as we walked the streets holding hands, watching the faces pass by. Not everyone in Ireland is pale and freckly. A lot of the women have rich, dark hair, almost olive skin and piercing eyes. They are some of the most beautiful women anywhere in the world, and that's Justine. My Irish lass.

Having said that, she did ask for a shot of raspberry cordial in her pint of Guinness at the rooftop bar of the Guinness factory. A most shameful act that I'm not yet ready to forgive.

I can't wait to go back to Ireland. Justine's best friend from school, Lauren Galloway, married an Irishman, Manus Hanratty, and they live in Dublin, although they do jump around the globe a lot. They're very dear friends, two of the very best, and we miss them.

Truthfully, I wouldn't need much of an excuse to get back there. It would be lovely to again witness that fading afternoon light, surrounded by the craic. I'd love to return to Ireland with Mum and Dad, see it through their eyes. Until then, I'll just have to make do with a pint at The Drunken Poet.

Thursday, 13 April 2017: Captain's run

For all the moments of spark and exhilaration in footy, there are days and weeks during a season when there is little more than the constant hum of routine and repetition. But then there are other days when the winds change or the compass turns, and everything sits in perfect balance under a golden glow of gentle, unexpected sunlight. It was one of those days today.

I'm in love with autumn. Certain cities are suited to certain seasons, and Melbourne is at its most beautiful when the leaves change their shade. There's something about the cool, crisp mornings when the winds lay low and the hot air balloons fly high that makes autumn my favourite time of year. If I ever leave this fair city to live interstate or abroad, it's probably the autumns I'll miss the most. George Eliot said, 'If I were a bird I would fly about the earth seeking the successive autumns.' I feel the same way.

For footballers, autumn comes at a good time. The playing year has begun, and the routine of the season is finding its rhythm. You can feel the cogs turning and the pieces slotting into place. Autumn mornings are enchanting, but by mid-morning footballers want the sun to have burnt through the clouds so conditions for training are note perfect.

All of this is swishing around in my thoughts as I drive towards Footscray for training, just after 7 am. I have grown to enjoy the daily toil and grind of football training. There's a certain type of physical poetry that comes with unrelenting routine, and that's what a football season is about: routine and then more routine.

But today I have an extra pep in my step. We've had a good week. After a surprising and disappointing loss to Fremantle in Perth, we're back on home soil and gearing up to play the Kangaroos in the very first game to be played on Good Friday. I have a good feeling about this week. Sometimes, you just know.

There isn't much traffic on the road and it's mostly going the other way, one of the blessings of heading west in the mornings. A triple-shot mug of coffee and You Am I blast me all the way to the Kennel – past the cemetery in Carlton and the Melbourne Zoo, through Kensington, up on the shoulder of the Flemington racecourse and across the Maribyrnong River. As I roll across the bridge, I think about the river's long Indigenous history and its connection to our club. This year's Indigenous guernsey, designed by Koori artist and Bulldog fan Kylie Clarke, incorporates a map of the Maribyrnong and the camping sites that were once dotted along it. Then I'm on the other side of the river, picking up speed, gently veering left towards the Whitten Oval on Geelong Road. I could almost make the trip with my eyes shut, I've driven it so many times. I have been known to head off along this familiar trail with Justine and the kids in the car when we're meant to be heading on a family outing somewhere else. Creature of habit.

The huge palm trees on the doorstep of the Whitten Oval come into view and I park my car. Today is 'captain's run' day – the last training session before game day. It is the least physically demanding day on our weekly calendar. In total, there will be four meetings for the morning. There's a different energy inside our football club for the captain's run. A respectful reverence. For what, I can't be sure. Maybe the battle ahead. There's nervous tension in the room. A few sets of knees bounce up and down as we listen attentively. One of those sets of knees is mine.

The irony of the captain's run at our club is that since I've become the captain, I rarely complete the session. I join the boys out on the ground for the warm-up and float through a couple of ball movement drills, but eventually I drift off to the side to watch while I rest my old legs.

The ten minutes that I'm out there with the boys are precious though. Your feet barely touch the ground on a captain's run. The fatigue in your legs from last week's game is long gone and you feel rested and strong.

Today, the stillness of the autumn air and the soft warmth of the morning sun allow everyone's skills to shine like diamonds. We're running on top of the ground. The coaches are relaxed, or at least trying to appear so, and the feeling in the group is that we'll win tomorrow. There's not even a hint of doubt. This is not how it is for other training sessions during the week; they have a gristle to them that is absent on the captain's run.

We take our time moving the ball from one end of the ground to the other, running among each other in big, sweeping figure eights, like ballroom dancers, and the ball glides across the oval before being rammed home for a goal – only for the dance to come back to life immediately for another run-through. I try to feel the ball in my hands, consciously feel the leather beneath the callouses, and carefully guide it down to my boot and sympathetically offer it up to a teammate who has led to space with outstretched arms. A perfect drop-punt pass that hits your teammate without him breaking stride is a precious moment. It never gets old. In the same way that if you let a bunch of horses out of the paddock for a gallop in the open spaces, some of them just shine a bit brighter than the rest. It's a joy to watch Marcus Bontempelli lope around the field. He's a special player. A thoroughbred.

There's a sparseness to the whole session, like the closing credits of a great film. For years I've stayed out on the ground for the full captain's run session, trying to soak in its goodness, but I can't do it anymore. It's hard to leave the group as they really hit their stride. But that's my lot these days.

At the end of a very light session, the coaches pick a spot on the ground and the players who have trained line up to take set shots at goal with the whole team and staff watching on. It's practice for the art of sledging as much as it is for kicking goals under pressure. Us oldies stand behind the goals and catch the footies as they fall in one by one to various degrees of cheering or jeering. There's five minutes after all of this to do any extra work the players need, and I quickly pick up a couple of footballs and go looking for my old mate Gia. We slip straight into the routine of kicks, marks and handballs from short range to sharpen up my touch before the big game.

On the surface, everything may seem relaxed and even laid-back, but it's not until the final tactical meeting (known as walkthroughs) is finished that all residual tension evaporates. The 22 chosen players stand out on the astroturf in position and we go through various scenarios that Bevo lays down for us. You can't plan for everything and the human battleships of footy can be a lot easier when you don't have to fight fatigue, but we feel prepared for the Kangaroos. The other business of the day is to acknowledge Travis Cloke's 250th game, and we adjourn to the theatre to watch a highlights package from his career. Pats on the back all round.

The work, if you could call it that, is done. It's 11.30 am and the rest of the day is gravy. I get my legs massaged, or 'flushed' as we say, by Roz Richards, our Welsh-Jamaican myotherapist, who I call Sis. She's my soul sister. I'm not sure I've met a more positive, kind-hearted or soulful person than Roz. She's a big part of the spirit in our footy department. But today we have a problem to solve. The daily riddle that is up on the whiteboard has us scratching our chins. 'When is a door not a door?' It takes Roz and I a good 15 minutes to work it out. 'When it's ajar.' The deflation of taking so long to solve the riddle is offset by the healing powers of the massage. I feel light on my feet and ready for the Kangaroos.

And then I'm done, free as a bird. I jump in the car, weigh up my lunch options and steer towards Seddon. I park, jump out of the car and run in to see my barber, Des. He assures me that if I come back in an hour he'll fit me in for a much-needed trim. Back in the car. Short trip up Charles Street to the Turkish café Advieh, where most of my teammates have congregated. It's a squeeze to get a seat, but I take my place among them and order my usual: mixed juice with extra ginger, a zucchini pancake on the side and a chicken wrap with chilli. The talk around the communal table is much the same as it's been for my 18 years in footy, and that thought alone warms my heart. I mostly just sit and listen. I only get some of the jokes. All teams have their own language or accent and these boys make me laugh with theirs. It's a simple life sometimes.

With a takeaway coffee in my hand, I say goodbye to the boys and it's not long before Des has me in the chair. Des has cut my hair for the last four or five years. He's originally from Manchester, his accent is still quite thick and he talks passionately about everything, especially Manchester United. Adorning his walls are posters of Oasis, Paul Weller and Richard Ashcroft. My bag, baby. He plays an eclectic mixtape of tunes on his stereo, but curiously nothing close to that resembling his posters on the wall, much to my disappointment. Just like lunch, I order the usual from Des: the only change from my last visit is the number of grey specks in my hair.

Des and I shake on it and I'm out the door again, and this time I'm headed east – though not for home just yet. I've got one more stop to make: Conway's fish wholesaler. The night before we play, I like to keep the menu familiar. These days it's a baked piece of Barramundi with ginger on a generous serving of risotto. If I'm eating fish, it's always from Conway's. They are the best. I walk inside and am greeted by Manny, whose family own and run this operation. They are big Bulldogs fans. Manny has a few questions about the team and I'm more than happy to indulge him. I sat in front of Manny at the MCG one day back in 2006; he wasn't as friendly towards the Bulldogs in the outer as he is to me and my teammates when we drop in to Conway's.

I tuck some salmon and barramundi fillets under my arm and hop back in the car, headed for home, everything in its right place. For the trip home, I pick the track 'Running on Empty' by Jackson Browne. There's something powerful about listening to the right song at the right time and this feels like one of those moments. It's a nostalgic lyric with a melody that's as pretty as hell, and its rhythm moves with momentum. The perfect road song.

I cross the Maribyrnong again, only this time I'm reminded of

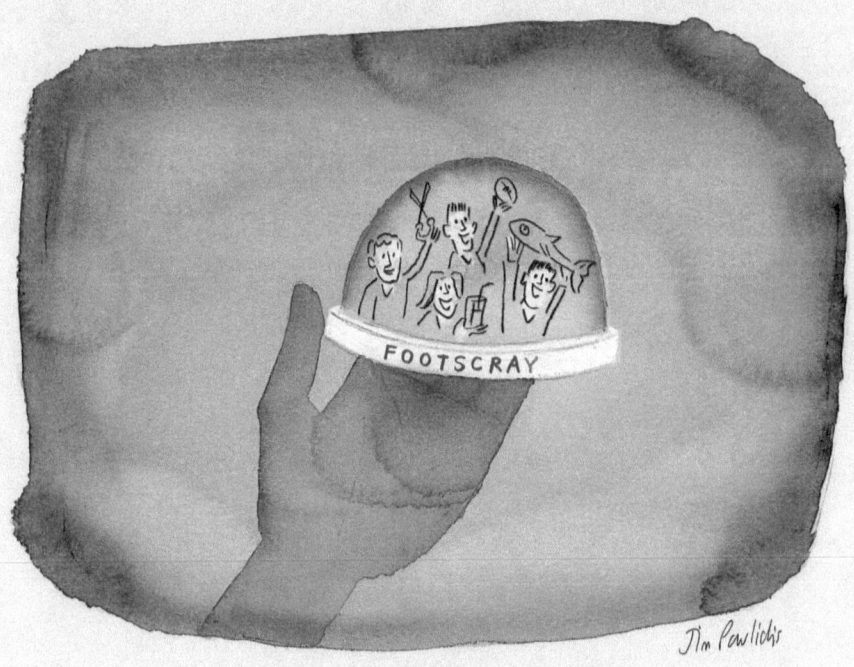

Terry Wheeler's speech from a couple of years back, when he spoke to the boys about the club's connection with the working class in the western suburbs of Melbourne. Decades ago, it was along the muddy banks of this river that tanners and blacksmiths worked long, hard days. And this is still a blue-collar part of town and we are still a blue-collar club. That makes me feel good. Proud.

A Springsteen song would probably work just as well right now, something like 'Factory', but the boy Jackson from California is about to find his chorus.

Looking out at the road rushing under my wheels,
Looking back at the years gone by like so many summer fields.

I'm picking up steam now, heading down Footscray Road with the bluest of blue skies high above me.

… Running on, running on empty
Running on, running blind
running on, running into the sun
but I'm running behind.

There's a metaphor in there somewhere. It's a fleeting moment of perfection, life in a perfect balance. But man, what a moment.

17

Blokes I Loved Playing Against

I like watching football with company. I enjoy observing how other people view the game. I've always been intrigued by journalist Martin Flanagan's preference to sit in the front row, peering over the fence so he can get a better feel for the pace and collisions on the field.

When it comes to watching footy, I'm my father's son. We watch players.

Our family barracked for Richmond and Peter Daicos, as contradictory as that might seem. I have strong memories of watching football at Waverley Park, the closest venue to our Warragul home, and a lot of those games (the ones burned in my memory anyway) were between Collingwood and Hawthorn. This was the late 1980s and early '90s, but even with all of those superstar Hawks running around, Dad and I weren't there to see them. Hawthorn was the enemy. We didn't like their colours and they always won, more than enough reason to dismiss them.

I liked Collingwood, but I didn't barrack for them. I think

that's what they call an oxymoron. It might even be deemed un-Australian in some circles, although I have an aversion to that term. We simply adored the balance, creativity and 'otherness' of Peter Daicos. He played the game differently to everyone else out there, and each movement or touch was full of thought. Those characteristics endure as the things I seek when I watch football now. With mixed results, I tried to play that way for the Bulldogs.

Daics was our man, but there were others. Dad would let out a spirited call of 'Wrighty!' every time the Pies' Tasmanian wingman Graham Wright broke free right in front of us and delivered a spearing ball inside 50. Dougy Barwick was an impact player whose physique and gait were slightly cartoonish. We loved him. Craig Starcevich was another that caught our eye, but this probably had more to do with him showing up at my school fete to sign autographs around this time, and because he was the obsession of Coodabeens' character 'Timmy from Thomastown'. The car radio was locked on the ABC on our trips down to Waverley.

It's easier to watch players as a neutral supporter, but the seed was planted in those early years. Even when I had more skin in the game in later years, watching the mid-to-late-'90s Tigers, I always followed the guys who thrilled me or made thoughtful decisions. Richo and Paul Broderick had all bases covered on that criteria.

My footy career was played from the flanks, both forward and back. The middle years were dedicated to playing as an undersized centre half-forward, but on official forms I always write my occupation as 'half-back flanker'.

One of the most enjoyable things I've experienced on the footy field was the vantage point of the half-back flank. For years, I got the best seat in the house and watched the game over the shoulder of some of the greatest-ever players. I got such a kick out of shadowing the movements of the stars, trying to tune in to their frequency and then attempting to nullify their influence while launching some meaningful play of my own. That's what I love about the flanks, particularly the back flank. It's a balancing act. Defend then attack, attack then defend. Punch or counter punch. From the flanks you often have to wait and see what the game does before unleashing your effort.

I played on Steve Johnson a few times, but there is one night that sticks out, from 2012. When I line up all the forward flankers I played on, Stevie J is the best. It's a tough call, a close one, but no-one squeezed more out of the two hours than him. There's lots of tiny little breaks in a game of footy, little moments of quick rest that dot the landscape like Caribbean islands. When you play on Stevie J those little islands are flooded. They disappear.

For example, we played the Cats down at Kardinia Park one day. Mitch Duncan took a mark close to the boundary line and went back to take his kick. This presented a potential island of respite, but Stevie just simply wouldn't allow it. His eyes darted around. He looked at Mitch, beckoned the ball with the whites of his eyes, which darted back at me to see if I was paying attention. Then up at the scoreboard, then over at Tom Hawkins. As those eager eyes flitted here and there, I could feel my little island going under, gurgle, gurgle.

The thing with Stevie that was often overlooked is how hard he worked. Everyone, myself included, was distracted by the tricks, those unorthodox moments of genius he was renowned for. But as a player he was so much more than that. For a start, he was big – bigger than you'd expect, and heavy too. Perhaps because his running style had a bit of a waddle to it, people didn't appreciate just how much ground he covered. He had extra time to show us his tricks, often because his opponents were struggling to keep up.

Then there was the chat. Our verbal interaction I wouldn't so much describe as 'sledging', more 'entertainment'. Sometimes I wondered if he talked to me on the field knowing that I'll pass the stories on to other people, which made him lift a gear. Suffice to say we chatted a lot out there, but he saved his best stuff for that night in 2012. It was my responsibility to take care of Stevie when he went forward, but if he pushed himself into the midfield I'd hand him over. By midway through the second quarter he was the most influential player on the ground, but I felt like I was having a good night too.

Just before half-time he waddled over to me, put his hands on his knees and let out a big groan. Then he said, 'I think I've almost halfway run this flu out.'

I knew what he was doing, planting the seed with me, 'I wonder how well he'd be going if he was fully fit?'

Just after half-time, Paul Chapman took a mark right on the 50-metre arc and went back to take his kick. I knew Stevie had been on the bench, and that he was now back on the ground, but I couldn't find him. I searched and searched in a state of growing panic. And then I saw him – standing next to the point post all on his own, arms waving madly. Mercifully, Chapman didn't see him either and put his shot through for a point. I found out after the game that Stevie had snuck onto the ground and run around the boundary line all the way to the goals as a disguise, then bobbed up next to the post as if he'd been hiding behind it.

When the ball was being ferried into the centre circle after a goal a few minutes later, Stevie again appeared next to me and with a wry smile asked, 'Did you see me come on the ground?'

'Clearly not,' was all I could answer, somewhat embarrassed and defeated.

'It was quite rascalish, wasn't it?' He was beaming, literally the cat who'd got the cream. But like all true performers, he saved his best until last.

Deep in the last quarter, when it was obvious to everyone – especially himself – that he was the best man on the ground, the ball was quickly kicked out of the middle in our direction. The game had tightened and was in the balance. I lunged to spoil, did a good job of it too, but the task was far from complete as Stevie scampered after the loose ball. He took possession with me in hot pursuit, right on his tail. He pivoted, and fired off a left-hand handball over his right shoulder to a running Joel Corey, who found a leading forward.

In terms of the overall result, it was a dagger to the heart, and this time I knew what was coming. Within moments Stevie was walking next to me, and uttered the classic line, 'I usually save that shit for finals.'

On Brownlow night, the umpires awarded the votes: Stevie J – 3, R. Murphy – 2. I'm quietly proud of that.

My longest-running battle from the flanks was with St Kilda's Stephen Milne. Milney kicked over 500 goals, a Herculean effort for a small forward. But he was more than a one-trick pony. He was a classic small forward in some ways, always feeding off the crumbs created by Riewoldt, Hamill and co. But he was also able to mark the ball on the lead, something that Eddie Betts also perfected. It's a great one-two punch to have and always kept me on my toes when I was minding him.

Milney talked more than any player I ever played on, including Stevie J. While he talked a lot, the chat never reached Shakespearean heights. One night Milney and I really went at it. At one stage he looked at me with total disgust and said, 'You've played 200 games and you're still on the half-back flank! You're a disgwace!' As if my career had stalled at middle management when I was really desperate to make it to CEO level in the midfield.

It's also worth noting that Milney and I are the same age, and at that point of our careers we'd played roughly the same amount of games. So I replied, 'You're a forward flanker and you've played 200 games – what's the difference?! It's a mirror image!' He didn't seem to get where I was coming from. As good a player as Milney was – and he was a bloody good player – I reckon I got the better of him over the long game. I don't know if he'd agree with that assessment – my small sample size says probably not!

'Disgwace' became a bit of a catchcry in the Bulldogs locker room after I'd told the boys about my night with Milney. At that year's Brownlow Medal count I looked across to the next table and there was Milney. Our eyes met, and he mouthed a single word: 'Disgwace.' I'm still not sure to this day if he was in on the joke.

Your job as a defender is to always defend first, and then if you're able to win the ball and attack yourself, go for it. That was definitely my job description for most of my footy life. I loved nothing more than turning defence into attack and taking off up the other end with running bounces and precise kicking that opened up the game. I loved having the ball in my hands. To see an opening or a free opponent and spear a pass in that direction was my bag, baby.

Over 312 games though, there's only one player I can think of that played on my mind when I had the ball. Cyril Rioli is an offensive weapon. A superstar. Quick, dynamic and full of creative dare. But it's his ability to chase players down and bury them with fierce tackles that sets him apart from the rest. Whenever we played Hawthorn and I had the ball under my arm, I was acutely aware of the presence of a shark in the water. Instead of solely looking downfield to split the Hawks open, half of my mind would be scanning all around to see the dorsal fin with 33 on its back.

The best example I can think of when the game dictated much of life out on the flanks, was a night at Etihad Stadium in 2011 against Melbourne. My magnet was next to Liam Jurrah's, he was my responsibility for the night. The first quarter was open and the pace was frenetic, with the ball being moved freely by both teams, but the Dees had the upper hand. When I say 'open', what I mean is that the whole ground was being used to move the ball, and because of that our defence had to cover a lot of ground. Holes opened up everywhere.

The boy from Yuendumu felt right at home with so much space to prowl around, and he left me in his wake a few times with superior timing and athleticism. He kicked two points in the first quarter and looked like he was ready to erupt. I may have underestimated him, and at quarter-time I was concerned about where our match-up might end. In the second quarter the Bulldogs clamped down, slowing the Demons' ball movement to a crawl. The open spaces Liam had relished like he was back home on the red dirt of Yuendumu were cut down to a quarter of the size. The Demons weren't able to move the ball sideways with any pace, and this meant my Bulldogs' defence was sturdy and full of numbers to help out when the inevitable bombed kick came in.

Two games of football were played that night. The first one might be described as bush footy – there was a sense of chaos and unpredictability, raw talent came to the fore, and the feel of the game was very instinctive. Some players can tune in to this random frequency, while others are born with it in their marrow. In the second game, the curved, chaotic lines of ball movement were replaced by a far slower game style. The lines became more defined. Gone were the free-flowing curves of open play, replaced by grids and corners. It was modern footy's human battleships, where the most organised and well-drilled outfit invariably wins the day.

I don't know if I've played on a more instinctive footballer than Liam Jurrah, and it saddens me that we didn't get to see more of this fascinating man from the centre of our vast land. There's a great line from soccer great Gary Lineker: 'Football is a simple game – 22 men chase a ball for 90 minutes, and at the end, the Germans win.' On this night, the Bulldogs played German-inspired football for three quarters, and the frustration in Liam was palpable as I stood next to him. As his frustration grew his work rate faded and I was able to drift off him and mop up where I pleased with easy kicks and running bounces.

It might be a stretch to use that single game as a pointer to why Liam Jurrah's brief but brilliant career was cut short, but I find myself pondering the thought all the same. Our game is still one played on instinct, but it's a balancing act. The strategic, human battleships of footy that are controlled from the coaches' box sit on one side of the scales, while on the other is the inner child. Not thinking, but feeling your way in the game. Chasing the ball, feeling the rhythm of play and injecting your talents.

A sizeable percentage of players are drafted into the AFL with the scales heavily weighted on the instinct side; the search for balance can take an entire career. I found this balancing act very difficult for a long time – and I come from Warragul, an hour away from Melbourne, and am the product of every junior pathway available to a young footballer. I can't begin to fathom the difficulty of balancing these things having grown up in Yuendumu.

In the paper the next day. it was written that I'd outclassed Liam, but I'm not sure that's fair. If the game continued as it had begun in that first quarter, it might have been a vastly different story. That's sometimes the reality of life on the flanks.

The two best half-back flankers I've ever seen play the game are Corey Enright and Luke Hodge. Enright was the complete package. Versatile, skilful and helped his teammates whenever he could. Flankers of my generation hold Corey Enright in the highest regard. He is our Bruce Doull. I suppose one could mount a pretty good argument that Hodge was a midfielder or a utility, but if I was picking a team I'd have him marshalling the defence. Hodgey is the best on-field leader I've witnessed up close. When I was playing on the half-forward flank against the Hawks, I'd often pay a bit of extra attention to what he was doing or saying, searching for anything I could steal and palm off as my own at a later date. The lesson I learnt from watching him up close was beautiful ordinariness.

With the ball 50 metres or so away up the field, being fought over on the ground of a stoppage, Hodgey would marshal his boys. Even that description is potentially overstating it, so ordinary and simple were his words. Hodgey would talk to his fellow defenders, but he wasn't handing them the secrets of the football universe. This was not a man with access to the footballing equivalent of the Dead Sea scrolls. No, all he would do is talk to them about where they stood. All of us – six Bulldog forwards, six Hawthorn defenders – would have our eyes on the ball, a kick-and-a-bit away upfield. Hodgey would calmly move his five boys around, just a metre here, a metre there, most of the time simply reinforcing that his teammate was in the perfect spot to defend. 'You're perfect there, Birch, stay on your toes.'

What was interesting was the effect this had on his teammates. They became engaged with him and each other, they were connected, and because their leader had reinforced to them that they were in the right spot, their confidence grew. They were able to play more instinctive football, knowing that the human battleships of the game were well placed to win out.

For opposition forwards, the constant chat and reinforcement among the Hawks' defence made you feel like you were surrounded. Beautifully ordinary, but here's the kicker: Hodgey was *always* first to react to the moving ball up the field. He could move his unit around with the flick of a finger, like a great conductor, but when the ball left the congestion of the distant pack, he had an amazing ability to read where it was going, leave his man, and impact the next play with a mark or spoil.

He brought a simple beauty to life on the flanks.

Friday, 11 August 2017: Western Bulldogs v. GWS, Docklands, 12-minute mark, second quarter (WB 28, GWS 35)

Marcus Bontempelli bursts clear from a stoppage on the half-forward flank and spears a pass to a leading Jack Redpath. As soon as the ball leaves the Bont's boot, I can tell he's put too much on it. Big Red is 6'4" (193 cm for the young kids), but instinctively I feel like it'll go over his head. I make my move.

I sprint as fast as I can to the open side of the ground as the ball flies past Red's outstretched hands. The GWS player Harrison Himmelberg is quick and I can feel him breathing down my neck as the ball bounces away from us at pace towards the boundary line. I love this situation. There's lots of things I can't do on a footy field (a list that grows by the day, when you get to my age), but I love this scenario, I love this stage: confined space, opponent on my tail, the ball not yet in my possession.

In days gone by, I would have known I was about to evade my man, but it's been a while. I can't get space with pure leg speed, so I slow down. This is something many people don't realise – sometimes the best way to get away is to slow down first, and then go! It's the change in speed *and* direction at precisely the same moment that makes someone difficult to tackle.

I can control both of our movements now – it's like a dance and I'm leading. Everything is frame by frame, slow motion, moment by moment. I shift down a gear, feel him just on my back.

There's only a breath of air between painful embarrassment and my football freedom. I take possession and shake my hips. I give him the shimmy. I take him one way, then the other, then the other. Left, right, left in a split second with every bit of juice I've got in my body.

He lunges, he's close, but I've put just enough space between us to wriggle free. I turn for the pocket. There's no space there, which is why it's the right spot – maybe, just maybe Himmelberg assumed I'd turn for space and safer ground, but I didn't.

I look up over my left shoulder and see the goal face. It's tight and closing, but something just feels right tonight. The rhythm of the play, the rhythm of my legs, the universe pulling it all together. My last thought, if you could call it that, is 'balance'. I hold the ball softly, swing my leg through and try not to kick it too hard. The contact is sweet, as sweet as a Mark Waugh flick through mid-wicket.

I know it's a goal as it leaves my boot. It's the most exhilarating feeling I've ever known. A clean, crisp, musical note. It might never feel this perfect again. The ball spins and arcs through the middle, and it's enough to bring people to their feet. My momentum carries me towards the fence, and before me is a sea of red, white and blue. The clan. My clan. They feel what I feel. We are one and the same for a brief moment in space and time.

I drag my fists back and forth, from them to me and back again. I want them to know I feel the connection too.

One last time.

18

Characters I Loved Playing With

One of my great frustrations as a player in the modern era was defending the criticism levelled at players from the average punter about a supposed lack of characters left in the game. It usually goes something like this: 'There's no characters left in the game anymore, you're all just *robots*!'

In 2012 I wrote a column for *The Age* about playing on Steve Johnson. It's the only column that people have ever asked me about; it seemed to strike a chord. I touched on this characterless criticism and offered up Stevie J as proof that the game still has its share of characters. I also posed the question of whether to qualify as a 'character' these days, someone has to play the fool.

Over the years, I've seen many characters come and go from the locker room. Most of them kept their best work inside the four walls of the club and away from the bright lights and the public. Most of them never felt the need – or the urge – to be extroverts. They were just amusing in their own way. Some of them never even knew they were characters! They were good players, all of them, but most of them weren't stars.

So here it is: my eclectic team of daydreamers, larrikins, eccentrics, nudists, blokes who are just a bit 'loose', a pickle, and at least one mute.

B: Tim Callan, Craig Ellis, Lindsay Gilbee

HB: Shane Biggs (C), Jesse Wells, Ben Harrison

C: Ed Barlow (VC), Isaac Thompson, Jose Romero

HF: Zephy Skinner, Jack Redpath, Shane Birss

F: Patrick Bowden, Aaron James, Nathan Brown

Foll: Ben Hudson, Leigh Harrison, Liam Picken

Inter: Lukas Markovic, Will Minson, Danny Southern, Daniel Giansiracusa

TIM CALLAN

Tim would be surprised to find himself in this team (he may even be surprised to find himself in this book), but that's because he's a self-deprecating kind of guy. Unlike most of this group, Timmy was never the clown, never the showman, and if he was nude at any stage it was because he was in the shower. Tim is perhaps the politest man I've ever met, but he played with a lot of grit and heart. He finds himself in the back pocket here because it was he who 'threw the dart'.

A Bulldogs tradition on 'Mad Monday' was to put the team poster from that year up on the wall of the pub, and one by one hurl a dart at it and hope for the best. The rules were pretty simple: if your dart hit a player, that player had to have a drink. If it missed the players altogether, you had to drink. If you missed the poster completely, you had to take a *big* drink.

The interesting part was when the player took the dart in his hand and stepped up to the line. Abuse would erupt from all around. The would-be darts champion found himself in a cauldron of nasty, occasionally witty, barbs.

In 2010 we were at the run-down (since closed) Buckingham Hotel in Footscray, and the boys were in full flight. I was operating as line judge when Timmy stepped up to throw his dart. For reasons I can't recall, the two of us got the giggles as the wall of unfriendly sound filled the room. Laughing and trying to hold on to each other to keep our feet, Timmy whispered in my ear: 'I've missed the poster two years in a row.'

With the line judge barely able to stand up and the dart thrower smiling broadly, he let his dart go. It arced gracefully through the air. A hush fell over the room. The silence was broken when the dart landed – in the carpet, just short of the skirting board. A tidal wave of dissatisfied laughter, clapping and chatter filled the vacuum of quiet.

Timmy and I went back into position as two drunks laughing uncontrollably and trying to keep each other upright. We stayed that way for quite a while.

CRAIG ELLIS

Craig was just about the best-looking bloke ever to play a league game, and he played 122 of them for the Bulldogs and Melbourne. Craig, who was affectionately known to his teammates as 'Horse',

'Overzealous Ellis' or 'Pickle', was a square peg in a round hole inside the conservative walls of the AFL in the early 2000s. Maybe that was why he and I hit it off so easily.

Pickle was interested in a lot of things. In the footy world, that can sometimes come across as not being 100 per cent focused on the job at hand, but Pickle had a curious mind that he followed like a hound that's picked up the scent. Well, maybe at times he didn't focus all his energies where they needed to be.

We were on the eve of a game against the Adelaide Crows one day and our coach, 'Plough' Wallace, called Pickle over to discuss his potential opponents. Pickle went into a pretty detailed appraisal of young superstar Warren Tredrea. 'He plays for Port Adelaide, Craig,' said Plough, visibly disappointed.

If Pickle ever wrote an autobiography, I'd buy the first copy. He's crammed a lot into his life. Free from the shackles of the football world, Pickle was residing in Monaco, last I heard, with his partner and their two young children. He likes to spend his time sunbaking and swimming off his yacht, or flying by private jet around the world. He's made millions selling bikinis.

Pickle.

JESSE WELLS

Jesse is so fabled he's like the Loch Ness Monster of the Bulldogs locker room. Stories of Jesse's antics have been handed down from generation to generation to preserve their truth. In short, Jesse was a Tasmanian eccentric.

He came to the club as an 18-year-old brumby – big, powerful and a little awkward. Prone to making grandiose statements in front of his teammates, Jesse once claimed to have jet-skied across Bass Strait. On another occasion, half a dozen of us stood in waist-deep water at the end of the indoor lap pool after a long and arduous swimming lesson. With no warning, Jesse informed us that he could swim 'at least two laps underwater!' A few sets of eyes darted around our small group until someone said, 'Go on, show us then.'

Jesse seemed genuinely excited about his hidden talent for hypoxic training as he put his goggles on and got settled. Deep breath in, deep breath out, under he went and off he took. Then up he came, like a giant humpback whale exhaling all that air and water into the air.

Jesse emerged *before the first flags*, maybe five metres from where he'd begun. As he returned to the group of stunned onlookers, he simply shrugged and said, 'I can do it, I just ran out of breath.'

LINDSAY GILBEE

Gilbs left school at Year 10 and had a passion for lookalikes and hitting teammates on the chest with right foot drop punts from 50 metres away. He was a sensitive soul who laughed a lot and made you laugh a lot. No-one cared more about his teammates than Gilbs. There are a few stories about Lindsay that do the rounds – mostly featuring questions he asked: 'Where is the Stawell Gift run?', 'Is Easter only in Australia?', that kind of thing. My favourite stems from the day we had to complete a series of obstacle courses on that infamous SOG camp in 2003.

In the most difficult section of the course you had to run down a steep and muddy hill and, when you got to the bottom, jump at a mesh fence that was hard to get your hands and toes into. The fence was quite high, and if you didn't time your jump well you'd have to go up to the top of the hill and do it all again. The stakes were high – you had to get your feet in that fence.

I was trudging along the other side of the circular course when I looked up to see Gilbs hurtling down the embankment. Fatigue filled his body and even the effort of watching where he was going was too much. By the time he looked up he was at the foot of the fence and crashed smack-bang into it.

Gilbs just looked up and groaned out loud, 'Noooooooooo!' It was my favourite moment of the whole camp.

BEN HARRISON

Harro was a courageous and versatile player at the Dogs and he was very popular. The boy from Devonport has got funny bones and he tells great stories.

On that same SOG camp where Gilbs couldn't get over the wall, we also participated in some good, old-fashioned sleep deprivation. Armed with an iron bar as a faux rifle, the SOGs dropped us off by the side of a dirt road late at night about 200 metres apart. Our instructions were to stay on guard and if you saw anything you were to use the phrase, 'Halt! Who goes there?'

We were left out on that road for almost six hours. When the 'exercise' was finally completed and we were all picked up by the bus, we swapped stories of our time 'on guard'. Harro held us captivated as the bus bumbled back to camp, with his account of seeing a figure by the side of the road. He wasn't sure what it was, he was so tired he couldn't be sure. Then the figure walked towards him in the dark until it was only a few feet away from him.

Instead of using our instructed method of 'Halt! Who goes there?' Harro sheepishly whispered, 'Hello …'

According to Harro, as soon as he spoke the image disappeared. 'It was a ghost,' he told us.

SHANE BIGGS

Shane was an entrepreneur aged 15, breeding and selling birds out of his parents' backyard. He also worked at the local fish'n'chip shop on weekends. The shop was owned by a Chinese family, and it was Shane's job to deal with orders and complaints over the phone. In Biggsy's words, 'I was basically bilingual.'

I found all of this out one afternoon as Biggsy and I lay on adjacent massage tables. We always seemed to be rostered on together and I would ask Biggsy stories about his life before he'd become a footballer. His adventures were always fascinating and funny. The Croydon Chronicles, I called them. The Bulldogs' premiership team of 2016 featured an eclectic mix of eccentric characters. Biggsy was the top of the class.

On the field, Biggsy goes quietly about his thing from a

half-back flank and you rarely see or hear much of him in the media. But in the locker room he's a force of nature. If Biggsy was a cocktail, he'd be two parts insomnia, one part seductive dancer, one part mainstream snobbery, all finished off with a twist of Phil Collins' hit 'Sussudio'.

I've named him captain because he captures the spirit of this team. He is a character! A total original. When people tell me there are no characters left in footy, I just wish they could have sat in front of my locker for the last three years and listened to Biggsy perform his avant garde take on locker room tomfoolery.

ED BARLOW

Ed's best year of AFL footy was his last. He came across from the Swans as a rookie list player who had versatility and a legendary aerobic capacity. He played eight good games in 2011 and, as he describes it, 'kicked goal of the century' when he smothered a ball, ran onto it and drilled it home. Unfortunately, we only had Ed in our colours for one year, because Rocket Eade was sacked and another rebuild was underway.

Born and bred in Bega, Ed is affectionately known as 'Cheese'. Cheese might just be the funniest bloke I've met in footy. Like Harro, Cheese just has funny bones. He's as dry as a biscuit and has a nasally drawl that makes whatever he says sound funnier than the rest of us.

At Dylan Addison's engagement party, there were half a dozen of us standing around having a beer and, for a brief moment, no-one had anything to say. Cheese, while looking out at the horizon, just said, 'Well fellas, I think we've made it.' If any one of the rest of us said that at that moment, it wouldn't have been funny at all. But because it was Cheese we fell about laughing. That's the power of Ed 'Cheese' Barlow.

ISAAC THOMPSON

A man whose time at the Bulldogs is barely a footnote in the club's history, Isaac was a lovely young bloke from Adelaide who could play a bit but was too small and too light to mix it with the big boys.

After his second year he was let go, and a couple of days later joined the players one last time for our footy trip to Las Vegas. On the second night, a big group of us headed to a nightclub called Rae's about midnight, and soon discovered that Rae's didn't get going until 3 am. Only in Vegas. We took our seats in a big booth, and apart from the bar staff not another living soul was in the joint. Morale was low and fading.

Someone made their way up to the bar and asked the waitress for a 'bottle of something' we could use for a drinking game while we waited for the party to fire up. About ten of us sat around this circular booth with this mystery bottle in the middle of the table. I remember it had sparkly gold flecks floating in it; I'd never seen that before. 'Vegas', I thought to myself.

We started a drinking game, I can't remember which one, and we were passing the time, getting tipsy, having a few laughs, pretty innocent stuff. I was sandwiched in between Darce and Isaac. Then things started to go awry. Will Minson was directly opposite us, and he was furious. He started jabbing his finger in our direction shouting, 'I can hear you blokes talking about me!' The three of us couldn't help laughing, and our laughter only became stronger when Will ruffled his own hair with both hands and chastised himself. 'I can hear three voices in my head!'

Over the next ten minutes, our table of ten dwindled to four. Some were off wandering around the club, which was starting to fill up, and at least three blokes were crying. On sober reflection, it seems we'd been drinking absinthe, although that hadn't occurred to any of us at the time.

Due to a lack of numbers, we had to call an end to the drinking game, and it was at this moment that Isaac Thompson leaned across and said to me, 'I don't know what all these blokes are crying for – I'm the one who's just lost my fucking job!'

Isaac Thompson: 0 games, 1 great line.

JOSE ROMERO

Jose was a hard man. He played combative football and despite his small stature he had a nasty streak too.

My first few years at the Bulldogs were Jose's last few, and what often happens in those twilight years is a softening of sorts that accompanies the knowledge that the war will soon be over. I'd heard lots of stories about Jose's intensity and sometimes gruff nature, but after my debut year he took a bit of a shine to me. There's a real warmth when we see each other now, and there was always a kind text message for milestone games.

For my very first milestone – my first game for the club – things didn't go exactly how I'd imagined. All the older players came over and shook my hand and congratulated me when Terry Wallace announced that I'd be playing. Being so new at the club, I knew much teammate bonding was yet to happen, that I had to earn their respect, and that the friendships I craved would take some time to materialise.

Having said that, I got a bit of a shock when Jose approached me with those serious eyes and firm handshake and uttered the words, 'Good luck, Patrick.'

ZEPHY SKINNER

Zephy once showed me a photo of his 'brothers' from back home in Noonkanbah in outback WA after the club had given him a week off to freshen up during one of Melbourne's bitter winters. At least a dozen kids, aged from about eight to 17, were standing in the red desert, all wearing Western Bulldogs singlets, and every one of them held aloft a huge lizard they'd hunted and killed. It was a stunning image, perfectly encapsulating the cultural divide this Yungngora man was trying to bridge. On the very same day Zephy showed me his holiday snap I watched as he ran laps on a freezing cold, windswept Footscray morning, while a coach 'encouraged' Zephy to run harder. I felt helpless and thought to myself, 'What in the world must be going through his head right now?'

When Zephy arrived at the Dogs, I'd heard a rumour he could jump over a man from a standing start. It was a party trick of sorts, but I never saw him do it. The thing I remember about Zephy that still makes me laugh is that every day I saw the boy from the Kimberley I'd say good morning and ask him how he was. And every single time he'd just say, 'Fucken tired, ay.'

JACK REDPATH

'Big Red' is a throwback to another time, what I'd describe as a classic footy club character. A mountain of a man with hands the size of pumpkins, Jack laughs a lot. In an AFL culture of manicured beards, acai bowls for breakfast and pilates for warm ups, Jack is a refreshing antidote. He's a larrikin, a bit of a rogue.

He's a carpenter by trade who grew up in Kyneton, the son of a single mum who works in youth detention. Jack has a tattoo on his ankle that reads 'SKEKKA' with a smiley face above it. Why?

'Got drunk with my mates back home when I was 18 and my mates were calling me Skekka that day, so we tattooed it on my ankle.'

'Was your nickname Skekka?' I asked.

'Only for that day,' was Jack's nonchalant reply.

Jack had endured a fair bit in his footy career even before he got to the Bulldogs, which explains his late start at AFL level. Two knee reconstructions before he was 19, gets drafted and carves out a promising career as a fast leading, powerful full forward who kicks goals and breaks packs. Then he does his knee again.

I take my hat off to Big Red. He's a much-loved bloke within the club and perhaps because of his big personality and unique backstory, it was obvious how much the locker room barracks for

Jack. Everyone wants him to do well. We want all our teammates to do well, obviously, but it's a bit different with Jack.

I would love to have played more footy with the boy from Kyneton, but that's the way it goes. A character, with character.

SHANE BIRSS

Birssy used to sit next to me in the player meeting room, and one day Rocket Eade was a few feet away from us, giving us one of his legendary dressing downs. It centred around the idea that in the big moments we didn't have enough blokes who stand up.

As the spray was building to a crescendo, Rocket threw a question to the whole group: 'Why does Shane Warne field at first slip?' I think most of us twigged that the answer was because Warney *wanted* the ball in his hands.

Next to me, quick as a flash, Birssy quipped back: 'Because he's a fat, lazy prick?' I think I stopped breathing. Amazingly, Rocket laughed harder than anyone in the room. He was always good at changing gears from serious to jovial in the blink of an eye.

Funny things happened around Birssy. He spins a good yarn, but his greatest off-field accomplishment remains one of my favourite memories from 18 years in the game. As a fundraiser, players used to perform a strip show for the supporters. It was back in the day when players stripping off their clothes for fundraising was a great night out for the whole family. Hmm. Lots of things haven't aged well in footy and a strip night at a casino nightclub to raise a few bucks is at the top of that tree.

Anyway, this particular year's Manpower night was booked for the Saturday night after a game against the Hawks at the MCG. The talk in the change rooms and coaches' box pre-game wasn't about the Hawks, it was about Shane Birss and a spray tan that had gone bad. Some people were angry, some were disgusted, some thought it was hilarious. The Hawks trounced the Dogs that day by 72 points, but in reality it felt more like 172 points. It was as dirty a day as any I can remember.

The Manpower night went ahead as planned, but we were ordered to be at the club by 6 am on Sunday for a searching training session. We were also told to write our own match report and give our individual performance a mark out of ten. To give that mark context, Nathan Eagleton gave himself 5/10 and he was our best player that day. He might have been our only good player that day.

At the completion of the dawn training session we all got up one by one, hungover, to fall on our swords with marks of 3/10 or lower. Then Birssy got up, his fake tan still glowing. 'I gave myself a 6/10. I thought when I was on the ground I did all right, but due to a lack of opportunity I spent most of the day on the bench.'

A deathly silence fell. The usually mild-mannered coach of the time, Peter Rohde, let rip. 'Birssy, you turned up to the ground FUCKING ORANGE!'

You can probably join the dots. A dud spray tan morphed into the greatest verbal spray I ever witnessed in less than 36 hours. Not bad going from the boy from Sale.

PATRICK BOWDEN

Paddy was drafted to the club in 1999, alongside myself and a bumper crop of players who played a lot of footy for the Bulldogs. He's one of my great mates outside footy. A multi-talented sportsman, Pat hailed from Alice Springs and is the son of former Tigers premiership player Michael and brother of Tigers stalwart Joel.

Pat probably would have made this team on the strength of his Elvis Presley impersonation, but Birssy wasn't the only one to have a bit of a nightmare over that Hawks/Manpower weekend. Unfortunately for Pat, he'd had a bit too much fun at the Manpower event and slept through his alarm. Pat woke in a state of panic, jumped out of bed, went to hit the light switch, missed the wall, fell, then hit his head on the bedside table.

Pat was the only bloke who was late to the 6 am training session, and when he finally arrived he was wearing his training tights inside out. Just prior to Birssy getting up to walk us through his best-on-ground performance, Pat piped up from the back of the room, 'Ah, Rohder, in my haste this morning I forgot to bring my match report.' There were a few muffled giggles in the room. 'Haste.' Now there's a word you don't hear every day in a footy club.

AARON JAMES

Aaron had what could only be described as a 'colourful history' before he got to the Bulldogs. Let's just say he was a bit of a ratbag. A prodigious sweater, Jamesy was on his last chance as an AFL player when he came across from the Tigers in 2001, and for the most part he was on his best behaviour as a Bulldog.

Cursed with a permanent furrow on his brow, Jamesy had to leave the pub one night because he made eye contact with a bloke across the bar who took his expression as a challenge for a physical confrontation. Jamesy pleaded, 'That's just how I look!' before slipping out the side door.

Over that 2001 pre-season, we had a 'bonding' session at a pub in Williamstown, which was essentially just a booze-up. Players and coaches were all there. As the day wore on, things got predictably looser. The jukebox started to fire up and Don McLean's 'American Pie' came on. By this point everyone was singing along, and Jamesy put his arm around me and started singing as well.

But Jamesy's lyrics weren't Don McLean's lyrics. He was singing into my ear about our teammates standing all around us, taking the piss out of them. Clothes, hairstyles, drink of choice, etc. The rhythm of Jamesy's words not only fit Don McLean's, they hit the same rhymes at the same time! It was the closest thing to genius you'd ever find on a 'bonding' day. I laughed so hard Jamesy had to hold me up, but for the life of me I can't recall ONE. SINGLE. LINE.

NATHAN BROWN
The most skilful player I ever played with. He's also my mate, I think. He makes me laugh, but I'm not sure he's that funny. He's odd. He

would have you believe he's very shallow emotionally, but he has a heart. What's also unexpected, perhaps, is that although he's a bloke who left the club for money, I would use the word 'loyal' to describe him. He fights for his corner, as they say. Everyone has that one mate – the one they have to constantly justify and explain their friendship with to other people. Nathan's mine.

He was great with the young guys when I arrived at the club and put a lot of time into us, although he almost cost Daniel Giansiracusa and me our careers at the annual club ball in 2001. Earlier that day we'd been thumped by Carlton at Princes Park and I was feeling even worse because I'd been one of the boys singled out by Terry 'Plough' Wallace for a poor game. The general mood of the room was pretty sombre as people sipped beer and wine at their tables.

Midway through the night, I was standing with Gia and Browny, and two tables away were Plough, assistant coach Phil Maylin and their wives. On our table was a bowl of toffees, and Browny joked that he might throw one at the coach. Gia and I laughed, not thinking he'd actually do it. Then Browny picked up a toffee and underarmed it at the coach. Gia and I were horrified, but mercifully the toffee skidded past unnoticed. Crisis averted, or so we thought.

Not satisfied with his first attempt, Browny picked up another toffee, and this time he rocked back onto his leg and threw it like a New York Yankees outfielder looking to run someone out at first base. Browny had a strong arm, and as soon as he let go of the toffee I knew it was going to find its target. The hard lolly cannoned into the side of Plough's head. Gia and I couldn't breathe and kept our eyes on the ground, too afraid to move.

After a few seconds we looked up, but Plough was already making for the door with Phil and their wives chasing after him. I never found out if he knew who threw the toffee, and I wasn't going to be the one to ask him. Nathan Brown. Loose.

BEN HUDSON (aka The People's Beard)
Ben might be my favourite-ever bloke to run onto the ground with. He was a warrior. For other players, sledging was a way of putting the opposition off their game, but I think Huddo did it to get himself going. When he wasn't verbally intimidating someone on a footy field, he could look slow and lethargic, but before you knew it he'd have singled some poor bastard out and come to life. He'd blow up like a lilo mattress!

We played the Tigers at Etihad one day and Huddo was stalking the centre circle, pacing back and forth like a caged animal, spitting words out like bullets from a pump action rifle. They were all directed at one bloke – Nathan Brown. Huddo knew I was mates with Browny, but they didn't know each other. I've never seen Nathan speechless like that before. Afterwards, he told me he was genuinely shocked by the ferocity of the attack from The People's Beard.

On another night, we were playing Richmond again, but this time it was a young Tiger who was on the receiving end of The People's Beard's verbal talents. He wouldn't let the young Tiger pup go, and kept telling him over and over in different ways how ugly he was. I started to feel bad for the kid myself, when out of nowhere the Beard looked at me and said, 'Mate, you're almost as ugly as Murph!'

I almost stumbled. Then I started laughing, so did the Tiger pup, and so did the umpire, who was a witness to the whole show. Now I'm no Japanese sunset, but neither is Huddo!

The People's Beard.

LEIGH HARRISON

Leigh is still a mystery to me. He was a beautifully balanced and skilful player who was on our rookie list for a couple of years in the early 2000s, but he rarely said a word. He was quickly given the nickname 'Whispers' – apparently even when he did speak, no-one could hear him. He was a bit too handsome for football; his androgynous looks were uncommon.

Back then, guys could just go to training and go home and not much more was asked of them; meetings weren't very interactive and there was no peer leadership program. You could slip through the cracks, especially if you wanted to.

Now Leigh *must* have spoken to people – surely? – but I don't remember ever hearing his voice. I was always curious about him, so one day I cornered him in the gym and said, 'You don't talk much, do you?'

I swear to God, he just smiled. As I leaned in, I *think* his mouth moved. But I didn't hear a sound. Whispers.

LIAM PICKEN

Liam doesn't talk much either. A warrior on the field, Picko was the Bulldogs' player of the finals series in the historic 2016 premiership year. He's an old-school kind of dude. I've always kind of seen him as a farm boy from the 1930s. Reserved, impeccable manners, a firm handshake, but with a lot of thoughts swimming behind those eyes.

One day Picko and I were sitting in the players' rec room. I was talking and Picko was pretending to listen while a couple of boys played ping pong. On a TV in the corner the latest current affairs were being discussed on some morning show. The impossibly pretty TV anchors went to a story about people smuggling, and the broader issue around borders and immigration. Picko, who had been silent up until this point, just threw his point of view out there like a farmer tosses grain for the chooks. 'For all the trouble this causes, they shouldn't let anyone in.' I was incensed. The red mist fell as I launched my most passionate left-leaning counterpunches.

After a few minutes we had to go back to training and left it there, but it played on my mind all day. I got to training the next day and made a beeline for Picko. 'You were just winding me up yesterday, weren't you?' I said.

'I knew you wouldn't be able to resist,' said the quiet, thoughtful farm boy.

Picken 1, Murphy 0.

LUKAS MARKOVIC

Lukas is one of the most decent men I ever played with; he has a generous spirit and a kind heart.

In the immediate years after his playing days at the Bulldogs, Marko worked as a mentor at Ladder, a youth homelessness charity that was created by former Bomber Mark Bolton. Marko and his colleague Ed 'Cheese' Barlow were quite the double act when they came out to the Whitten Oval to talk to the players about the work of Ladder and how a player might get involved.

Marko's introduction went like this: 'Good afternoon, everyone, my name is Lukas Markovic and I work as a mentor for Ladder. I used to play here at the Bulldogs and now, as you can see, I've been in a pretty good paddock.' It was a lesson in winning over a group of tired footballers. Top marks from the judges.

WILL MINSON

I love Will like a brother. In fact, we fight like brothers. We argue constantly. No-one has asked more questions in the history of the game than Will. He just has to be in this team. He's a character. As a young player, Will was quickly pigeonholed as a German-speaking, saxophone-playing jazz appreciator, an image he helped create. But he is so much more! Wilbur is a Reebok-pump-wearing, ice-cream-making, SAAB-driving, fly-fishing, herb-growing, plane-flying behemoth! And that's just the tip of the iceberg.

This would never happen now, but one of the things that used to take place with draftees was that at the Christmas party drinks at someone's house the new kids would have to stand up and either tell everyone about their first kiss or sing a song. No-one ever sang a song. But when Will stood up, I kind of knew we'd get something different from the ordinary routine.

With a thick, private-school South Australian accent, he began. 'Well, there was this party, and I was standing out in the front yard with this girl that I liked, and we were just chatting, and I wanted to kiss her, but it all fizzled out so I just went back into the house and I made myself a sandwich.' Stunned silence.

Because Will had moved into my neighbourhood I knew he was a bit 'out there', but I don't think the other boys knew just how far. They soon found out. To this day, many of us still call Will 'Sandwich', or the 'The Big Sandwich Eater'. Pronounced 'Sarn-dwich'.

In 2010 Justine and I had a two-year-old and a newborn. We were tired, had no social life, and had very little time for anything other than getting through each day. I was getting a massage from our massage guru, Marcus Sinfield, in Fitzroy, and as usual Will had the appointment right after me.

Will walked straight in as I was putting my kit back on in a semi-zombie state, getting ready for the next round of punches from life. I asked Will what he'd done on his day off.

'Well, I spent the day searching Melbourne for different flavours of schnapps.'

I shit you not, he had spent an entire day pinballing around Melbourne looking for variations of a particular German liquor.

The Sarndwich.

DANNY SOUTHERN

Danny and I crossed paths for only a single year, but boy was he a character.

Danny finished up mid-year in 2000, my debut year. At the end of that year, the footy trip was to Thailand, and on one of those days someone decided we should go and play skirmish in the jungle. It was a terrifying experience, and not just because there were paintballs whizzing past my head. During one of these 'battles' someone came across a snake. I was over the moon. Not to see the snake, but because the fighting was called off while someone went and fetched our resident reptilian expert 'Southo'.

We all crouched down around the not yet fully grown snake. I don't think I was alone in expecting a Steve Irwin–style education session from Southo, but the mood changed suddenly when he stood back and emptied the rest of his paintballs into the poor reptile. Dead snake.

'Put your goggles back on, boys,' Southo said with that mad grin. 'It's skirmish time!' Gulp.

DANIEL GIANSIRACUSA

Before every game I ever played at AFL level, I would make my way over to Daniel Giansiracusa to complete a small marking and handballing routine. In the beginning, it was just to sharpen up our touch and reflexes before a game, but over the years it morphed into something else. For me, it became a symbol for all the things my dear friend had taught me: work ethic, attention to detail and the importance of routine. Towards the end of my career, I began to think about this routine as being like a football prayer. It was only finished when Danny kicked the ball into my hands and I took it cleanly 13 times. That was his number, that was my tribute to him, although I'm not sure I ever told him that.

If this team should ever pull on a jumper, as unlikely as that is, I just need to know that my great mate will be there alongside me. We were drafted on the same day, spent the first year as rivals (a rivalry that never let up, we just added the warmth of friendship to it). He made me better and I owe him a lot. Danny was a smart and creative footballer, a hard worker and a damn good wet-weather footballer. He's going to make a great coach one day. The number 13 is considered unlucky by some. Not by me.

Saturday, 19 August 2017: Dreary Ballarat

The great Brent Crosswell once wrote in *The Age*, 'Give me 80,000 people at the MCG and I was Hercules. But give me a grey day at the Western Oval and I wasn't worth a cracker.'

I wonder what ol' Tiger would have made of lining up in search of four points on Mars? Mars Stadium that is. That's this week's mission – taking on Port Adelaide at football's newest venue with our finals hopes more or less on the line.

Ballarat is the Bulldogs' new home away from home, and the club is hoping it can become a fortress in the way that Launceston is for the Hawks. It certainly felt like Launceston when we arrived by convoy last night. It was freezing. There's been talk all week about the potential of snow in the area at this time of year, and as we stood on Mars Stadium familiarising ourselves with its dimensions, it was easy to believe snowflakes would flutter to earth any second. It really was that cold.

After a wander around and a brief address from Bevo, we all hopped back in our cars and headed to the team hotel for dinner and a massage. I could feel flu symptoms coming on, and that miserable winter's realisation was accompanied by a bout of the blues. This game is hard enough, particularly at 35, without having to battle the fatigue of man-flu to boot. I took some Nurofen and was tucked up in bed by 8 pm, hoping that by morning I'd be right to go.

I awake to the sound of rain and feel as flat as a crepe.

Heavy thoughts flood in. 'Today is going to be a tough day.' But it's never a matter of, 'Will I play?' You just push through and try to find something. Coffee, paracetamol, adrenaline and the sight of Dale Morris getting ready to play with a plate in his broken forearm do the trick, and eventually I'm ready for Port Adelaide. I don't need to be best on ground, but I need to be out there, doing my bit. Pointing and yelling, etcetera.

By the time the ball is bounced, I feel good enough, but with a tricky breeze and a tough opponent it's a scrappy game. Not that the crowd seems to mind; they're happily getting into the swing of having an AFL game in their hometown.

It's no classic, far from it, but the scores are close and there's plenty of feeling. But I'm not having a great time of it – I don't have much spark or turn of speed in my legs this week. This is a hallmark of footy for the ageing veteran: some weeks it's there and you think you're holding back time. Then the next week, mysteriously, it's gone again.

I can't find much space and I'm frustrated. Every chance I get, I take the opportunity to get under the skin of Port defenders, trying to psych them out. It's a pretty childish pursuit. At one point the game opens up and I have Port defender Tom Jonas off side. Matt Suckling kicks the ball out in front of us, more like a soccer-style through ball than a pass. I take off after it and get excited that I might be able to ignite something in the game. The crowd rises with the excitement too, but as I take possession Jonas brings me down immediately with a good tackle.

Genuinely surprised that he was able to keep up with me in the open field, we scrap it out on the ground and I knock the ball out to a teammate. As I'm lying down watching the footy pinball between players, Jonas rubs the back of my head, pressing my face into the ground. I see red. As the play leaves our area we jog after it, but I'm seething and the Bulldogs supporters behind us know it. I feel the alien urge to throw a punch at him. I've never felt that in my entire football career, so why now?

The disturbing truth is it's because I'm embarrassed – the game has passed me by, I'm out of tricks and I'm desperate.

Instead of a punch, I run up next to Jonas and slap the back of his head, Basil Fawlty–style. For the first time in my life I see myself as the typical old country footballer, desperately hanging on, not ready to let go. It's not a pleasant image. Jonas and I engage in a war of words and I take a slight points victory when I seem to cause genuine offence by telling him I don't even know who he is. It's a lie, but it's the only card left in the pack for a 35-year-old to play when he's being beaten on the ground and on the scoreboard.

I bury all the thoughts of sadness and embarrassment deep down. I'll get to them later. For now, I've got to keep the pedal down, and I spend the rest of the day being beaten by various opponents and shooting my mouth off. It's all under the guise of 'sacrificing for the team', but does it really help? I'm not so sure.

Just before half-time, I get a lucky free kick in the forward pocket and the siren sounds as I'm picking myself up off the ground. I do my best Matthew Lloyd impression and throw some grass high into the air. A strong right-to-left breeze lets me know I need to aim at the right goalpost. There's a lot riding on the kick. We're six points up. A two-goal buffer will be worth gold in a low scoring game. Because of my verbal tactical agenda today, there's also a bit extra riding on the outcome of my set shot.

I line up, begin my approach, and hit it sweetly. The breeze going across my body moves the ball a grand total of 15 centimetres over its 30-metre journey, and it hits the right post flush. I look at the post with the disgust of a golfer whose putt has lipped out of the cup. And here they come. Hamish Hartlett wants a piece of me. 'You got what you deserved, because that was a lucky free kick.' I come right back with, 'It's not just the people of South Australia who think you're a total cunt.' I think my verbal escalation shocks him. It certainly shocks me. His response only heightens my inner embarrassment. 'I actually said nice things about you this week after your retirement.'

Not my finest moment.

As we settle into our half-time meeting to listen to Bevo's address, I feel completely empty. All that wasted energy trying to be a standover man, combined with the flu, has left me a spent force. I'm worried what my output could be in the second half. I spend my time taking big breaths, in and out, trying to calm down.

The second half goes much like the first: scrappy football with a bit of spite and plenty of verbal arrows being fired across enemy lines. I've found a bit of spark and run, and with scores level I take off on a daring run up the middle of the ground, take a handball from Caleb Daniel with a sense of excitement about what I might see up ahead, but to my disappointment there's nothing much at all. So I fire the ball off to Luke Dahlhaus to buy us a bit more time before attacking again.

As I watch my handball drift through the air, Port midfielder Brad Ebert comes out of nowhere and hits me with what used to be called a shirtfront. It's a classic hip and shoulder, but the force of the bump causes my neck and head to whiplash and we clash heads in the chaos of bodies colliding. I go down. I stay down.

The doctors get to me and ask, 'Body or head?' My reply is an encapsulation of defeat. 'Everything.'

I manage to get myself up and walk from the field, a small cut on my cheekbone all there is to show for the brutal hit. I pass any concussion concerns and put myself back into the fray. The season is on the line, but there's a part of me that doesn't want to give Port Adelaide the satisfaction of finishing my day. I wonder, is that competitiveness or pettiness?

In a metaphor for our whole season, when the game is in the balance our boys can't find that extra gear and Port can. They run away with it in the last six minutes to win by three goals.

That's it. Our premiership defence is more or less done. A whole range of mathematical equations need to fall our way to get back in the top eight now. It's been a dirty day on Mars. This whole season has been hard work. The energy of the last two years just hasn't been there this year. The magic we had disappeared. I don't really have an answer for why that is. Everyone seems a bit jaded. It's been a massive cultural shift that just can't be denied. Our club's identity for so long has just been to survive. We had one premiership cup in the cupboard from 1954 and chasing the second one was a bit like trying to land on the moon for JFK's America. When we did it, before anyone expected, with an unorthodox team, it caught everyone off-guard. Especially ourselves. When you land on the moon, where do you go next? The 2016 premiership was different to other clubs winning a premiership. Hawthorn, for example, are mountain climbers, each premiership is just the latest summit. They have a culture and expectation of winning premierships. Of scaling mountains. The Bulldogs culture was to dream about premierships and endure hardship. When we landed on the moon we weren't quite sure how to move forward. That's my rationale anyway. The next great challenge of my football club, the Bulldogs, is to become mountain climbers and not astronauts. We need to keep our feet on the ground and breathe the clean air under the atmosphere. Our culture is changing. Evolving.

None of that makes me feel better, though, as I drive down the freeway headed for home with more tears rolling down my face. The thudding realisation hits me in the chest again. I won't play in a premiership, there will always be a hole in my heart as a footballer and I have to brace myself to carry that for the rest of my life. As I pull into my street and limp through the door, I receive a text message from my friend, ex-Bomber, Mark Bolton. The message reads 'Footy ... shiving people in the kidneys for over 100 years'. That about sums it up.

19

Leadership and All That

I get a cold sweat at the thought of someone thumbing through the pages of this book to 'the leadership chapter' in the hope of getting some pearls of wisdom. I don't have the answers. The only thing I'm sure of is that my style of leadership and specifically how I approached the captaincy was different from the style of those who had gone before me.

In 2008, on a pre-season camp, former Essendon and Geelong ruckman John Barnes remarked that I was neither a leader nor a follower. I thought it was an accurate judgement at the time. But I evolved as I got older. By the time I took over as captain in 2015, I was a leader. Unashamedly so.

I had some good fortune when I took on the job. Foremost in that was the fact that I was 32. I'd been around the block a few times. I had life experience under my belt. The bruises of poor choices and broken trust had become companions to lean on. I knew all about the anxieties of the professional footballer and I thought I could help young players avoid some of that wasted heartache. I've come to know there is a big difference between 'how are ya?', and (with a gentle hand on the arm) 'how are *you*?'

The intensity and scrutiny of the game tightens and magnifies every year, both internally and externally. This rising temperature must be offset by empathy and tenderness. I think the public would be surprised by the level of love and care inside professional football clubs these days.

If there's one question I loathe being asked above all others, it's 'What kind of leader are you?' That's just not for me to say. Ask the people I was supposedly leading. When people talk in too much depth about leadership styles, I feel nauseous. If pushed, I suppose my style fell under the banner of authenticity. I just tried to stay true to myself, or a better version of myself. That was pretty hip for a while, until it was overtaken by 'agile' leadership. Who knows what the next fad will be?

I prefer practical descriptions of leadership, behaviours I can touch. I remember before the 2007 AFL Grand Final watching in amazement at how relaxed Geelong captain Tom Harley was in the rooms. He seemed completely at ease, and you got a sense his players felt that calmness too. The Cats won by 100 points that day. I tucked Harley's calm into my top pocket. I built my leadership nest, as it were, like a magpie. A bit of this and a bit of that.

I heard Sydney Swans captain Brett Kirk accept an award one year. At first, he talked about leadership in a fairly stereotypical way, but then his language changed and it grabbed my attention. 'You've got to play with discipline and lead by example. And when the shit hits the fan, you're knee-deep in it.' Yoink. I'll have a bit of that.

And over a cold beer in front of my fireplace one night, my dear friend Paul Yeomans half-jokingly quipped, 'Manage with facts, lead with charisma.' Now, I'm not suggesting for a second that I was any more charismatic as a leader than the next bloke, but my observations were that the good leaders all had something innate. They were naturals and they had self-belief. Scott Wynd had it, Luke Beveridge and Terry Wheeler too. I tried to steal what I could from them and others.

I was at a fundraiser for St Kilda City footy club recently, on a panel with ex-Tigers Michael 'Butch' Gale and Matthew Richardson. We were opposed by musos and thespians – Tim Rogers, Tex Perkins and Rhys Muldoon – with Brian Nankervis as MC. At the halfway mark of the evening, Brian asked Butch if he could recall any memorable half-time speeches. Butch told a story about him and his older brother, Brendan, riding pushbikes for 20 minutes while listening to the eccentric rantings of Tasmanian coach Froggy Newman. Apparently, on this particular day Froggy was in a ferocious mood. He lambasted his players for not showing enough guts. Then he reached into a bag and pulled out a possum. In a show of brute gore, Froggy ripped the possum open with his bare hands to illustrate the guts he wanted his players to show. It was quite a tale. Brian, like the rest of us, giggled with shock and amazement, before moving on with, 'I suppose we can just be thankful the possum was dead.' Butch leaned in to my ear and whispered, 'It wasn't.'

Froggy's method is a long way from how footy teams and their leadership operate these days. It speaks to the blunt force that permeated much of what was considered leadership back in the day.

The other stroke of good fortune I had, of course, was having Luke Beveridge as coach when I took on the job. I think I could only have been captain under Luke; we just seemed to fit. Our styles were heavy on love and empathy. No animals were harmed at our football club in the years between 2015 and 2017 – but we weren't the Brady Bunch either. Although there were plenty of hugs and tears during this time, it was no hippy commune. I sat across the table from Luke many times to tell him when I thought he'd missed the mark, and they weren't easy conversations to have. I lost count of the number of times as captain that I had to have a word to a player about unacceptable behaviour or not meeting training standards. As a young player, I avoided that kind of conflict, as many young players do, but I understood it was part of the job when I took on the captaincy. And of course, in the spirit of balance, I had my turn on the other end of it and had to listen, absorb and improve.

One of the things that emerged when I became captain was loneliness. It would come and go. It's a common situation for the captain and other leaders to feel caught between two worlds. On the one hand, it was our job to hand down the coach's message, support it and drive standards. But we also had to take on what the players wanted and needed, and deliver that back to the coach, whether he wanted to hear it or not. I was blessed to have a leadership group of the highest calibre. Having experienced warriors like Dale Morris and Matthew 'Keith' Boyd at my side was a luxury most captains would kill for. They helped shoulder the extra weight of responsibility.

You could hypothesise for hours about what led to the Bulldogs winning the premiership in 2016, but one of the things I come back to is the emotional alignment of the club leadership at that time. Peter Gordon as president, Luke Beveridge as coach, myself as captain, Easton Wood as vice-captain standing in for his injured skipper, Marcus Bontempelli as the best player and Lisa Stevens as our club psychologist – all vastly different people, but I thought then, as I do now, that all of us, in an emotional or spiritual sense, pointed in the same direction. A better way to describe it might be that each of us played a different musical instrument – trumpet, piano, cello, etc. – but we all played from the same sheet music. I think we laid down a soundtrack that was easy to follow. It was a tune that told a story, with simple symbolism that centred around doing your bit for someone else as well as fulfilling your own obligations. We had heart, but we demanded that everybody was 'all in'.

Leadership inside a football club is not a destination you arrive at. It's a Rubik's Cube that's constantly changing. At times, I felt like I had ten fingers and there were 11 holes in the boat. Most of the time you feel like you're falling just short of how you want things to be.

I've joked with people in the corporate world that a football team as a business model is a disaster. Having 44 players and only

22 spots in the team each week is not great figures for harmony. And then you throw in the fact that at the end of *every* year there will be redundancies. Good luck!

At its most basic level – and I came back to this thought again and again – leading the Bulldogs was about asking, 'How can I help?' Sometimes the help was a hug, sometimes it was a shove. There were times when I knew I had to take charge, and other times when I felt it was best for me to stand back and wait for others. Oh, and for all of the philosophical jargon, it does help if you can get a kick. As captain, you don't have to be the best player, but your effort cannot waiver. And you must accept that at times you'll get it wrong. If you're that person who flicked through this book looking for the answers, the cheat sheet would probably read: When in doubt, ask yourself one question: what would the great Carlton captain Stephen 'Sticks' Kernahan do?

When all's said and done, the captaincy and all that falls under the banner of leadership crystallised for me in the final moments before we played the game. The calm before the storm of competition. Leading the players out onto the field and then bringing the boys in tight around me to talk matters of the sporting heart – that was the greatest thrill of my sporting life. All the hurt, responsibility and euphoria of a life in the game was bundled up around 22 men that day, bound together by the unpredictably of what would happen next. Would it be enough? Would all of those little deeds and efforts be enough? The one certainty we had was each other. That's how leadership felt to me.

Friday, 25 August 2017: Hawthorn v. Western Bulldogs, Etihad Stadium

In all likelihood, tonight will be my last game of football. It's a strange feeling. Martin Flanagan once said 'athletes die twice'. It's a line that I have thought about a lot. It's pretty heavy stuff. In a rather unusual build-up for my last game, I've been attacked by Sam Newman on *The Footy Show*. It was a stinging verbal assault. Basically, he accused me of stealing the limelight on Grand Final Day last year. I didn't watch the show, but it's blown up and a lot of people are having a say about it in the media. It's embarrassing, hurtful and I just don't have much energy to go up against it. How can someone be so cruel? I knew that I couldn't please everyone during that time last year. I was determined not to sulk in the corner, so I fronted up, supported my teammates and celebrated my club's great day. And why now? Almost 12 months have passed since that day. I understand that football is a bit like the jungle, every so often, something or someone leaps out to take you down, but this feels like a king hit. Talk about the saloon door hitting you on the arse as you leave! I can hold a grudge as well as anyone and as I prepare for my last-ever game of football, part of me wishes I was anywhere else. I don't think I can ever forgive Sam for that. And yet, there is a job to do. A job I have loved. I try and slip into the old routine one more time and finish off with a dignified performance among my boys in our colours. One more fight.

Preparation: The smell of eucalyptus always gets me in the mood for a fight. I think that might almost qualify as a Pavlovian response. Minutes before every game I've ever played, I've made my way into the trainers' room and stuck some Vicks up my nose. It's about putting on the armour. In those final few moments before you take the field you morph into a different character. What some people call 'white line fever' takes hold, but it looks and feels different for everyone.

The fever doesn't turn everyone into Robbie Muir or even Glen Archer, but it puts you on edge. The fight-or-flight response fills your stomach and stretches out to tingle your fingers and toes. Your mind walks the high wire between loneliness and a deep sense of brotherhood. You're a gang. The feeling is precious and pure.

The change rooms are quiet, but I can hear the frenzied noise of the masses in the distance, just beyond the concrete walls. Time moves like glue as the anticipation builds. To pass the time I pace the room, slap my hands together, put an arm around teammates to offer some words of comfort. I press resin into my hands and spread it around my palms so the ball will stick in my grip.

Despite the tension and storm clouds on the horizon, I try to keep a calm facade. I'm our oldest player, the captain; maybe the younger ones will look to me. I've learnt that our boys play better when they're relaxed. I try for an easy smile to ease some of the tension in the room, but inside I'm like a pinball of thoughts, hopes, fears.

Someone gives the signal and we come together briefly with Bevo. He gives us a final message. It doesn't really matter what he says, it's the symbolism of the picture. We are his boys. He's with us. We break the tight circle and turn for the door. The noise grows louder.

I get to walk out first, and the sense of pride and privilege never gets old as I look back on the team we have. My boys. Our support crew and a few ex-players line the walls respectfully as we leave the rooms and begin our ascent to the field. It's the greatest feeling in the world. I walk slowly up the race, savouring the moment. Gradually picking it up to a jog as the field of play comes into view, we explode onto the ground as a team and our clan rise as one with us. Our theme song comes from the old sea shanty, 'Sons of the Sea', but we are the Sons of the West, and our tribal hymn blasts out across the stadium. We are snarlin'. You can't touch us now. This is our childhood dream, and we're all living it.

When I can't play anymore, I know in my heart that it's these precious seconds that I'll miss the most.

20

The End

There was a theory put to me that the overarching theme of this book would only emerge once it was almost complete, and I now believe that to be true. Looking back over these pages, I see many arcs. It's a bit like chopping down a gum tree to find the rings in the timber. Spheres of time. Innocence arching all the way around to experience. A few knots of imperfection for good measure.

I'm 35 years old and my life can be easily split in two: the innocent, sensitive kid and the professional footballer. A couple of things have emerged out of this pursuit, for me anyway. One of them is the result of two opposing forces smashing into one another. My childhood was almost bereft of strict rules and schedules. As a schoolkid, my only real practical use for time and a clock was the understanding that I had to leave the house when the microwave read 8.21 am. If I walked out the door at precisely that time, I would meet my school bus as it rounded the bend. A minute later, and I would have to walk all the way to school and risk being late.

Jim Pavlidis

I was, in some ways, quite bohemian for a teenage boy with a bowl-cut hairdo in a conservative country town. I was free. I went from that freedom, and some lanky running for the Colts, straight into the cut-throat system of a professional football club. Rules, uniforms, routine and then more rules. It was a shock. Professional football clubs can feel like the army in more colourful uniforms. I took a while to find some breathing space in its confines.

If my childhood and upbringing were easy, my football career, was anything but. Every team, every player in the league, is always trying to prove a point, and I suppose I was trying to prove that I could endure. Was I tough enough? Playing on in 2017 was clearly about one last chance at a premiership, but more than that I wanted to show people I could come back from a knee injury at 34 and still mix it with the best. Who was I proving a point to? I'm not sure. Maybe myself. I feel content that I ran the tank dry. With the petrol light blinking away, I took this beaten-up body around for one last ride in the sport of kings. I don't regret that for a second.

One of the rings in the gum tree was the draftee who nestled under the wing of the elders of our club at the time. Guys like Luke Darcy, Simon Garlick, Craig Ellis, Ben Harrison, Nathan Brown, Todd Curley and Matthew Croft guided me with a firm but steady hand, and gave me shelter from the storm. When I became an elder myself, I was caught off-guard by the paternal instincts that awoke in me, and it was under my wing that I could provide similar refuge for the next generation. I gave young blokes like Easton Wood, Jordan Roughead, Luke Dahlhaus, Jack Redpath and Jackson Macrae everything I had and everything that had been handed down to me. The lineage of the locker room and the battlefield.

I was lucky to play alongside good men for much of the way. Maybe as a reaction to my gypsy-hearted ways, I gravitated to blokes who you could set your compass by. Daniel Giansiracusa and Matty Boyd were like my north stars for years. A focal point to keep my ship on course. I always felt a sense of comfort walking up the race and seeing those guys next to me. That's almost the highest accolade a teammate can bestow on another, I reckon.

I've always been a fan of the great players. I got to play with so many, but Chris Grant and Marcus Bontempelli stand out. Complete players. Stars. That's something to tell the grandkids. For all the nonsense in the analysis of the game, most of us still acknowledge that the special ones move differently. Something in the nuances of their play sets them apart from the rest of us.

Granty's ability to pick up the flight of the ball in the air and mark it in front of his eyes with perfect timing – with danger all around – always left me feeling lucky to have such a close vantage point. Watching the Bont create a path in the chaos of play with his big frame has already become a trademark. Playing alongside him, I could hear the appreciation in the outer from our own supporters. It was even more graceful from a few feet away. With the ball in his hands he'd lope away in slow motion, like he was wading through waist-deep water, the sea of stragglers falling away in his wake, one by one. A football Moses. Or Jesus. Definitely biblical.

Right now, in late 2017, my future connection to the Bulldogs is a little unclear, but monthly pizza nights with the Bont and our manager Tom Petroro are enough to fill my belly and Bulldogs heart. It's not very rock'n'roll to hang out with your manager I suppose, but *your* manager isn't as cool as ours. Tom is a good man to have in your corner. If they make a sitcom about our pizza nights it might be called 'Two Italians and an Irish stallion'.

If you play for long enough – and I was blessed to play for a bloody long time – the relationship with your club changes. For a time, your footy club is who you play for, and then at some point that club is a part of you and you are a part of it, linked forever. Like family. I love the Bulldogs. It might read as a throwaway line, but it's a love that I would never mask behind any sort of ambiguity. Footscray and the Whitten Oval will always feel like home.

I have much to be grateful for, not least the chance to actually play, but one thing that jumps to mind is the notion of loyalty. It's seemingly a fading currency in professional sport, or so I'm told. Loyalty in sport isn't dead, just a little misrepresented. It's not *blind* loyalty. Too much is at stake. The loyalty I've known in footy is a relationship – there must be an exchange of effort and goodwill. The Bulldogs and I were a good couple. I gave them everything I had. I hope they feel like they got a good deal, too. I'm a proud servant of the Bulldogs. Forever.

This book was never going to be titled *Murphy*. I wasn't that sort of player, and I didn't have that kind of career. For a long time the title I had in mind was *A Footballer's Lot*. Much of this book is a collection of stories of *a* footballer. That footballer just happened to be me. There were many other titles …

I suppose it would be good manners to tell you that I never saw myself writing a book and that this 'just kind of happened', but that's not true. After being encouraged many years ago by one of my heroes, Martin Flanagan, to write a different kind of footy book, I set my coordinates to doing just that. My hope was that this book would fill a gap. As a footballer, I was neither a champion nor a notable disgrace. The risk was that I wouldn't have a story to tell. That in itself I found interesting, the notion of writing a footy book that shone a light on the middle ground. The highs and lows of a life in footy, the feel of the bumps along the trail from inside the middle of the pack.

Then I became captain of the Bulldogs. A young football team caught fire, a club emerged from obscurity, and then something else happened. I'm still not entirely sure what that 'something' was, but I know it involved a lot of hugging. I don't know if we changed the game, but for a brief moment the Bulldogs were hip. There was a story.

It's funny, but I'd never felt a part of my generation before that time. Even when I was a teenager at the underage disco, all the kids were screaming the words to grunge anthems like 'Smells Like Teen Spirit' and 'Killing in the Name'. Plenty of the kids were from broken homes; they meant it, they felt the songs in a way that I didn't. I was secretly hoping the DJ would play Van Morrison's 'Brown Eyed Girl'. I enjoyed an angst-free world. A charmed childhood.

Regrettably, I spent much of my footy career either writing or daydreaming about footy, music and clothes from another time. Living in a daydream, a cartoon world of nostalgia. And then my football club was thrown into crisis at the end of 2014, and I woke up. My three years as captain, I felt alive. I felt present. All the chips were on the table. There was a sense of desperation and defiance in the air. It was a 'damn the torpedoes' kind of vibe. Every moment felt important. It was an exhilarating ride.

During the low ebb of October 2014, one inescapable thought kept throbbing in my head: 'My football career has meant nothing.' It was a depressing thought. Fifteen years of getting to the line and the club was ultimately in a worse place than ever. And then something magical happened. I look at those last three years as a trilogy. The rise of '15, the glory of '16, and the struggle of '17.

I described the 2016 premiership and 'that' medal moment with Bevo as being like a mountain in my life. But just like Uluru, the colour of the mountain changes in the light. On most days I see a beautiful landscape. A football fairytale rising out of the ground pointing towards the heavens. But there are other days too. There are times when just the memory of that day and that moment break my heart in two. Even now, I still brace myself when a stranger starts up a conversation with me about the premiership or the medal. I'm scared of what they might say. It all depends on the shade of the mountain on that day.

A memoir like this demands a level of candour. It's only recently I've come to accept that my greatest day in football was Grand Final Day, 2016. But I must also acknowledge that my worst day in football was the very same day. I am both proud and ashamed of that fact. As a leader of the club at that time I was so proud, the euphoria was so real. But I'm also a footballer and on that day I was not where I was meant to be. I felt that in my marrow. I will never get over it. For a time, *Almost* was another title option, but its black humour might have been too obscure. On those blue days, it helps to remind myself that despite the twinges of heartache, they are nothing compared to that sense of being unfulfilled in 2014. I sit back now knowing that, at least, it meant something.

When you join a club, you inherit its history, its mythology. There's been a heavy load to carry in that regard if you chose to be a Bulldog. Survival and fightbacks aside, our one shining light was the premiership of 1954. It was so long ago that the only footage of the day is fuzzy and incomplete. A bit like a football Zapruder film. *Back and to the Left* is another good title option now that I think of it. That premiership and its mythology grew over time, and the walk to the Footscray Town Hall became something of a spiritual pilgrimage. These stories were glorious, but weathered, aged.

I felt at the time that the 2016 premiership healed a lot of the pain of our football club. Since 1954 there had been so many losing seasons. Too many. The history books give us the ladder and the checks and balances of the wins and losses, but those columns don't accurately record the emotional damage all of that losing causes. Too many people have left our footy club unhappy or bitter. There was something special about the 2016 team that brought a lot of people back and seemed to rekindle the love and attachment people once had for the club. All of us who spent time at the club since 1954 had daydreamed about what it might look like if we won the flag again. What would a sea of Footscray supporters at the Whitten Oval look like the day after the battle was won? The reality was better than our dreams; how often can you say that in life?

After the historic presentation of the cup to the Bulldogs people at our home ground, the inner sanctum of the club and their families came together at the Railway Hotel in Yarraville. That was special too. So many beautiful people. So many characters with big hearts. That team, that finals series, felt like a shooting star. Magical. I was privileged to be among them. On the Monday, just the players reconvened at the same pub and things were, as you'd expect, pretty loose. It was still early in the day when I thought, as the oldest player, that a speech should be made.

I stood on a stool, pint in hand, and talked about the significance of history. I opined that some of the players with a medal around their neck might have some comprehension of what they'd just done, and maybe some of the older ones would have an even broader appreciation. But I told them to leave a bit of space for the possibility that it was even bigger than they thought. This premiership, for some long-suffering Bulldogs people, means they can actually die happy. I got down off my stool, content that I'd nailed it, and Matthew Boyd sidled up next to me. 'Bit fucking morbid bringing dead people into it, don't ya reckon?' I'll miss that about footy clubs. Brutal truth.

Someone asked me recently what life was like having just retired from the AFL, and I told them it was a bit like leaving the *Big Brother* house after 18 years. The hyper-focus the game demands is now gone. I can feel some tension leave my body. It's a tension that has been present for a very long time. I remember hearing players who have retired over the years describing retirement with the same line, 'The war is over'. They're joking, but there was always some obvious truth attached to the joke. Post-war, I'm now trying to find a new rhythm. It's a rhythm that is both physical and mental. In many ways, a footballer's life is simple because you work and then recover, work, recover, and that is the backbeat to your whole life. The days of the week now all feel the same. There's no real change because the weekend isn't anchored by the physical anarchy of a game of football. It might take a while to find my new drumbeat.

I am, as I write, sitting on a fold-out plastic chair under the annex of our rented Winnebago in a caravan park in Byron Bay. The heat is tropical. We left Melbourne three weeks ago and we're headed for Port Douglas. All up, it'll be two months on the road by the time we leave the van and fly home. The 'Holiday Road', as it were.

The first time I visited Byron Bay was back in the early days of the millennium, and it had a big effect on me. So big, in fact, that on my return flight home I landed at Tullamarine wearing a sarong. Yes, I was *that* guy. For all of the trinket shops, burning incense and faux spirituality, there is an undeniable energy around these parts. The centre of town is almost a touristy imitation of what it once was, but there's magic in them there hills that surround these pretty beaches. You can feel the life in the air and see its vitality in the dirt. I've been back to Byron Bay every year ever since. There's a small town about ten minutes inland, called Bangalow, that Justine and I have had our eye on for more than a decade. It's our 'one day' place.

Right now, the sun is starting to fade and we've opened a bottle of wine. The kids have gone in search of bitumen adventures on their wheels of choice. I'm sitting like my dad and my son, cross-legged and in the shade. I look down at my legs. It's been almost three months since I last ran out as a player for the Dogs, and it's starting to show. Both of my knees are lined with scars. The physical toll of the game has left harsh slashes across my flesh.

Dermott Brereton once said that if you played more than 200 games of league football you had a daily reminder through some kind of physical ailment. He's right, of course, and I limped to 312. Both of my knees ache a bit when I go for a run these days, but I manage well enough once I get going. My toenails are yellowed and gnarled like bamboo from years of punishment, and the hint of a gut is starting to show, but it's my neck that gives me the most grief. A 'popped' disc in 2010 did the damage and it's never fully recovered. Uncomfortable as these ailments are, they're badges of honour too. I gave the game a pound of my flesh. There's no comeback on the cards.

If I look back again inside the circles of the fallen tree, I see two kicks. The first, a wobbling, floating mongrel that came off my boot in my very first game against the Blues at Princes Park, and went dead straight to put us in front deep in the last quarter. That glorious line turns all the way around the wood until it comes to meet itself some 18 years later. My last game of footy. With the game tightening, Lachy Hunter feeds me the ball and I see space in front of me. My heart lifts as I sense the moment. I could turn this game on its head, bring us back into the contest with a running shot from just inside the 50-metre line. I swing my leg through and it makes the sound of a bum piano chord. It could very well be the worst kick of my career. Off the side of the boot and into the stands, I get the Bronx cheers from the Hawthorn supporters. It's my last-ever touch in a game of footy.

Just ten minutes ago, in this Byron Bay caravan park, a father and a son were having a kick of the footy on the tennis court. The ball flew off course, over the fence, and rolled a few feet away from me. I stood up excitedly and moved over to shoot a handball so the kick-to-kick could resume, but my thumb caught my pocket and the ball limply fell off my forearm and rolled into the fence. I looked up and the dad quipped, 'Bit like your last kick!'

My last kick was the kick of a man whose best days were long gone. I was done. If I were a racehorse at that point, they would have pulled the white sheet across and destroyed me at the track. If I'd kicked it sweetly, post-high through the middle, I might be sitting here wondering if I should be playing on. But I'm not. I don't want to play anymore, I don't have it in me anymore to get to the line. That's a relief. I'm sure there will probably be little moments where I'll long for certain things, pine for the contest or the chase, the sweet kicking musical moments, but that's life. I had my time.

And it was a wonderful time. I was the kid who played the game in the street until dark, yearning, dreaming of what it might be like to actually play in the big league. And I did it. It was harder than I thought it would be, much harder. But to quote Tom Hanks in *A League of Their Own*, 'Of course it's hard – it's the hard that makes it great!'

I wasted a school education wondering what it might be like to play on the MCG in the fading light of an autumn Saturday afternoon with the game in the balance, and I did that. It was beautiful. Better than I could have imagined. The game hardened me, thickened my skin. For all of my idealistic babble about being a kid free of stress and full of adventure, I was a young adult that was almost bankrupt when it came to accountability. That can wear people down, and I wore a few out. The game beat some reality into me. Taught me about discipline and responsibility.

That's what *Leather Soul* is all about. A young, naive kid, with a brand-new football in his heart. Over time, the leather aged from the bumps along the trail. The elements of Footscray winters and some glorious liniment-scented afternoons. All of the laughs, the scraps, the yarns and characters. The game. They all left a mark on me, on my soul. I wouldn't change any of it. Not one thing. That was my lot.

This story is also about a girl. I adore my wife. Part of my adoration is that she is still something of a mystery to me. I never tire of her, although I know she must tire of me. Athletes are famously self-absorbed and often lost in their own thoughts. I've been accused by my wife on more than a few occasions of not being 'present'. Recently, I was talking to a well-regarded journalist's wife about this very thing and she told me, 'Writers are the worst! They're always off in their own worlds, ignoring the real world, the real-time problems of life at home!' Now spare a thought for Justine, who has married a now ex-footballer who wants to be a writer, but really wishes he was a musician. Blimey. The girl deserves a medal. I'd give her the Jock McHale medal, but it's in the Bulldogs Museum now. And it's not mine anyway.

Praise from Justine is hard-won, and this forms at least a small part of my infatuation with her. Once, I decided to bring a bit of 'peer feedback' home and into our marriage. It was a mistake. I know that. Now. I said, 'On the count of three, let's describe each other in one word. Okay?' Justine agreed, without hesitation.

'One, two, three.'

Me: 'Honest.'

Her: 'Lazy.'

I believe they call that 'checkmate'. How could I wriggle out of that?

For all of her talents for cutting through my bullshit and her 'honesty', she loves me and we have a great life. Of all the arcs in the timber of this tree, the one I love the most is the one that starts at a swimming sports carnival in 1995 and just keeps spinning. If I dropped a needle on that line, it would play a beautiful tune. In terms of my football career, I know I won't be remembered as a winner, but I got the girl. So, I win.

This Winnebago idea up the east coast has been scaled back. For a time, I wanted to move the family to an Italian village for six months. Then it was Galway on Ireland's west coast. For a little while we considered driving across the USA. Finally, we decided that the closest we could get to 'total freedom' would be to avoid airports and hotels and drive a home on wheels north. The trip was quickly dubbed 'freedom in a cage'.

When we pull out of this caravan park tomorrow morning and head for the tropics it won't exactly be like a Springsteen song. This ain't a '69 Chevy. But we'll be pullin' out of here to win, baby.

Afterword
by Gerard Whateley

'I don't get the Bob Murphy thing.'

It was said in the company of a thoughtful group of sports writers – those who seek the nuance and fable of the endeavour, above the blunt force of result and associated outrage. Given the prevailing disposition of the group, the sentiment seemed incongruous. Yet a clever colleague quickly seconded it.

Burying a creeping sense of offence as an acolyte of the 'Bob Murphy thing', I saw an opportunity to explore the idea rather than object. Why were Bob's columns treated with such reverence? What insight did they truly offer beyond the typical current-day player pap?

A quick reference to the Stevie J. column brought a collective smile to the group. The column in which Bob surrendered his premiership dream and reset the purpose of his twilight years drew instant recognition and a nodding sense of approval. You were left with the sense we'd strayed into 'What have the Romans ever done for us?' territory. It became apparent the objection wasn't to the essence of the work, but rather the aura that had built around it.

The mistake was to see Bob as the way and the truth in football rather than the road less travelled. At a time when footy hurtled towards crass, brash saturation, Bob was a counterpoint offering a spiritual connection and insight into the game. It was unusual and unique. It came through a curious journey. His were never the markers of mainstream popularity. When the skinny rookie penned 'No War' on his arm for an official team photo, the Coalition of the Willing he conscientiously objected to was broadly popular. It's believed there's a well-worn Kevin07 t-shirt in a drawer somewhere. They weren't the obvious choices for a footballer's calculated cause celebre.

His column in *The Age* began as an offbeat endeavour, not an appendage to a burgeoning profile. He was Robert then. And he developed a select following.

He was an intrigue when he came to the *AFL360* desk. The ambition was to stage a weekly conversation between two players, rather than the prevailing interview format.

He connected instantly. Soon enough he was Bob.

He talked about footy in a different way, effortlessly blending a depth of emotion with a light touch. An even greater accomplishment, given those were the tortured years.

As if to emphasise how utterly unplanned it was, Bob brought 'rascal' into the footy lexicon. Rather than calling Hayden Ballantyne a prick for punching an unsuspecting Paul Chapman in the guts, Bob curiously reached for 'rascal'. He felt he'd never used the word before in his life. It stuck. And with a little encouragement morphed into a celebration of the lovable, playful aspects and characters of the game. Steve Johnson was quintessential. Jack Riewoldt the heir apparent. But the least rascalish person in the equation became the one saddled with the moniker.

At the risk of overreaching, his *AFL360* days changed Bob's football experience, or at least his relationship with the football community. For those of us who crave connection and understanding, he filled our cups. He could articulate what we hoped to be true: that the game has a greater meaning. He could convey the menace of being hunted by Cyril Rioli. He could distil the essence of the madding crowd. *Weak as piss Simpson.*

The scope of his appeal may have been limited at first, but fascinatingly Bob became something to everyone – to such an extent that he won the *Herald Sun* fan poll for Most Popular Player year after year.

The reason? We all saw Bob as we wanted to. We overlaid our own ideals and made his image fit. He was our football laureate. It probably wasn't fair on him, but he was the hero we needed.

This collective attachment to Bob heightened the tragedy of the knee injury that denied him the premiership every fan wished for him. Collectively, we felt a seething sense of injustice. As Bob did his duty, we demanded he articulate *our* pain.

Every camera lingered too long. The external misery cast him down an impossible path. One which he walked with a distinguished stride.

Sam Newman's vile heart couldn't comprehend it. Singer-songwriter Paul Kelly's gentle soul understood it perfectly: a man had never been so present in his absence.

At the end, we loved him for the grace, style and skill with which he played. He fulfilled Mike Sheahan's early comparison to Robbie Flower.

We revered him as a leader – a Pied Piper who elicited loyalty through word and deed and reinforced the honour of the struggle.

And ultimately we are indebted to him for making us believe in the game again.

Gerard Whateley

Acknowledgements

I had a lot of help writing this book, unashamedly so. The team at Black Inc. / Nero not only supported me, but they also inspired *Leather Soul* with their maverick spirit. Caitlin Yates and Kirstie Innes-Will, in particular, pushed me along to make it the best book it could be. We wanted to create a different kind of footy book, something original, and I think we succeeded.

This is my book, I wrote every word, but some dear friends have gently influenced these pages like perfume with their questions and thoughts. The campers, the swivellers, @presentationnight, Tex, GW and PK all chipped in. RH helped with some advice and Jim Pavlidis contributed illustration wizardry. Thank you, one and all. Sincerely.

For lots of reasons, I hope this book sells a boatload, but the main reason is that I want it to be worth Peter Hanlon's while. Peter is technically my editor, but he is so much more. I describe him sometimes as my liniment comrade. I worked him hard on this project, let me tell you! *Leather Soul* just wouldn't work without

Peter's wisdom and honesty. I love him. He's one of my heroes.

You're not meant to meet your heroes, at least that's how the old saying goes, but that doesn't ring true for me. I only met Robbie Flower a few times, but each time I was left shaking my head, astonished by his gentle, easy manner. And his lack of ego, in contrast to so many of his '80s contemporaries. A sweet man. A hero to any skinny bloke who has ever pulled on a jumper. His loss stung; I wanted more time with him. I've kept his business card in my wallet as a token of our brief friendship.

Matthew Richardson and Wayne Campbell, along with a few of my other Tiger heroes, have always been generous to me. They indulge all of the questions and fascinations from my teen years. They're just my mates now, I guess, and that blows my mind, but I still hold on to some of that little kid's awe and wonder. I think they secretly get a kick out of it too.

I'd heard the name John Schultz when I was drafted to the Bulldogs, but I had no idea of the man's aura and his endless dignity. While so many of us try, try, try to be heard, try to be of some use by writing books, talking on radio, smiling on TV, John just walks around quietly, shaking hands and treating people well. He has had more of a positive impact on the game than all of us peacocks put together. An absolute gentleman. He's the best.

Is it a cliché for the youngest child to want to impress their older family members? Cliché or not, I fit into that category like a foot fits into a sock. I wanted to play well to make my family proud.

Mum's adventurous spirit runs through me like a mountain

stream. Mum sings, paints and tells good stories. She's a country girl at heart – tough and resourceful. During various Bulldogs crises, she gave me pearls of wisdom. My favourite was: 'Don't wait for the wind, grab the oars!'

I don't really have a parenting philosophy, but if I did it might be, 'What would my sister Bridget do?' Bridget and Souma have five beautiful kids (Jimmy, Joe, Billy, Fred and Daisy) and they live a life full of heart, spirit and generosity. What else is left after that? My perfect Saturday night would be to sit in their front yard in Inverloch, light the fire pit and listen to Souma's stories. The life and times of Ben Soumilas, now that's a book I'd buy. Souma might just be the best-kept secret in country football in Victoria. He understands people and the game. That's a good coach.

I wouldn't have played one game of AFL footy if it weren't for my brother, Ben. He toughened me up as a little kid and put thought into the way I played. My first football memory is being placed in front of my older brother as my cousins kicked the ball high above my head. Ben would scream 'CAPPER!!!' and wrap his legs around my head as he attempted mark of the year, over and over again. My first favourite song was 'He Ain't Heavy, He's My Brother'. Ben was my protector. Not much has changed. What's the test for a relationship? One that I adhere to is: if the shit hits the fan, will you be there for each other? If Ben and Steph and their children, Emily and Hugh, need me, I'm theirs.

Reflecting on what's in these pages, I can't ignore the gentle role that my father played in my football career. Dad and I watched the stars of the game from the outer at Waverley Park and I took him with me onto the field as I got a closer look over 18 years with the Bulldogs. It might be a long bow, but I felt like he was with me as we watched all the great players from this era within arm's length, and for brief moments I teased at being a great player myself. I hope Dad feels like that too. Whatever I was on the field, I offer it up to Dad as a gift for cleaning my boots every Friday night.

About the author

Bob Murphy played for the Western Bulldogs for 17 years and was their captain from 2015 to 2017. In 2015 Murphy was named captain of the year at the AFL Players Association awards and was also captain of the All-Australian team. The following year, the Bulldogs won their first premiership in 62 years. Murphy has written regularly for *The Age*, and his first book was *Murphy's Lore*.

www.ingramcontent.com/pod-product-compliance
Lightning Source LLC
Chambersburg PA
CBHW030102170426
43198CB00009B/464